This book is dedicated to anyone on a journey of recovery

One of the most important daily rituals at Restaurant Sat Bains is the staff meal. Each day everyone from the kitchen and front of house sits down in the early evening before service begins to eat together. It may be lasagne, roast chicken and vegetables or even some really good sausages and mash. This is a meal we prepare every day, side by side with the dishes to be served in the restaurant.

Most importantly it's a ritual that brings us all together, where we talk about our day, aspects of the business or even ideas about food and wine. What we've come to realise over the years is that this one ritual is the thing that binds us together. As well as feeding us all and getting us ready for evening service, it brings us together as a 'family' where everyone has a voice and a place. It's when we can all offload and laugh together. It's great for morale and communication.

The routine of preparing and sharing food together goes further than just nutrition. It brings a sense of balance into life and daily routine.

The importance of Helen's book should not be underestimated.

Sat Bains
Michelin starred chef and restaurateur

Contents

Contents 8

Foreword 12

Preface 13

Our senses 14

Thoughts and feelings 16

About this book 18

Healthy tips 30

Lunch and Light Bites 34
   Morgan's omelette 36
   Cheese scones 38
   Cullenskink 41
   Rustic pea and ham soup – with a twist 42
   Beefburger 44
   Potato pattie 47
   Chicken satay kebabs 48
   Stuffed mushrooms 51
   My mum's chicken drumsticks 53

Breads 54
   Basic bread dough 58
   Bread sticks – gluten free 60
   Brioche 61
   Challah 62
   Chapatti 63
   Linseed bread 64
   Focaccia 68
   Naan 69
   Pitta 70
   Pretzel 71

Mains 72
   Fresh salmon and mixed vegetables 75
   Saag aloo: potato and spinach curry 76
   Corned beef hash 78
   Fish en croute 81
   Cottage pie 82
   The Italian meal 84
   Mushroom pizza 86
   Bacon, liver and onions in tomato sauce 88
   Tuna pasta bake 91
   Chicken curry 92
   Lasagne 94
   Chicken, lamb or mutton moghlai biryani 96
   Jollof rice: the soul food! 100
   Grandma's stew with Yorkshire pudding 105
   A fisherman's breakfast 106
   Seaside fish pie 109

Jerk chicken with rice and peas 110
Grandma's bubble and squeak 115
Salt fish and ackee 116
Mince and tatties 119
Chicken masala 120
Beef stew and dumplings 122
Chicken korma 124
Dad's shepherd's pie 127
My mum's Sunday dinner 129
Corned beef pie 131
Mutton curry 132
Authentic lamb kebabs 134
Chicken chow mein 137
Fishcakes 138
Chicken tajen with lemon preserve and green olives 140
The pattie in the sock with gravel lot 143
Cawl – Welsh stew 144
Bangladesh lamb curry 147
Panag 148
Rustic Kashmiri curry 150

Puddings and Desserts 152
Chocolate cake with silver 'ball bearings' 154
Blackberry and apple crumble 156
Fairy cakes 158
Festive chocolate cake 160
Nana's bread and butter pudding 162
Banana loaf 164
Chocolate and orange marble ring 166
Mixed fruit crumble 168
B's banana bonanza 170
Rice pudding 173
Auntie Mickey's cheesecake 174
Malt loaf 178
Boobelach 180
'Depression cake' – pineapple upside down cake 183
Gran's treacle tart 184

Extra Things 186
Auntie Mickey's cheesecake: gluten free and lower sugar version 188
Sage and onion stuffing 190
Pease pudding recipe 190
Dumplings 191
Rice and peas 191
Yorkshire pudding 192
Conversion charts 193

More thoughts and feelings 195

Where the recipes come from 196

Glossary and interesting stuff 198

Acknowledgements 204

This is Nottinghamshire Healthcare's second book which features food.

The first book, *Positive about Healthy Eating*, was published in 2009. It was originally designed as a health and nutrition resource to aid the health professional when working with their patient group. This book went beyond fulfilling its objectives and has become universally used – by individuals, as well as within public, private and third sector organisations.

This new book is warm, inviting and friendly; it is designed to provide an insight into some of the key issues that face the Trust's patients, service users, carers and staff members within its care settings today. There's a story in it for everyone to identify with. This book is timeless – you will be able to keep it forever!

"If we could give every individual the right amount of nourishment and exercise, not too little and not too much, we would have found the safest way to health."
-Hippocrates

About Helen

Qualifying as a chef/cook and specialising in classic and Mediterranean cuisine began a lifelong interest in food, good nutrition, health and well-being.

In 2004 my work at Rampton Hospital – the high secure psychiatric hospital in Nottinghamshire – focused on weight management programmes for patients with related physical health problems.

After gaining a teaching qualification, I began work as a lecturer in the Hospital's Further Education Centre where I tailor-made a healthy eating cookery programme, endorsed by the Open College Network (OCN), which I delivered in consultation with patients' medical teams. Whilst continuing to lecture in Healthy Eating, in 2008 I embarked on a Master's Degree in Nutrition and Dietetics at the University of Nottingham.

My first book, *Positive about Healthy Eating*, adopted as a model by Nottinghamshire Healthcare in 2009, stimulated staff and patient interest in a cosmopolitan range of healthy option recipes.

In 2011 I had an exciting opportunity to be seconded to write a second book, collaborating with patients, service users, carers and staff within Nottinghamshire Healthcare.

Nourishing: Recipes and Reflections on Recovery is the end result.

Foreword

I am happy to support such a wonderful book that calls on people's memories of food and how those links with the past, family, friends and eating together can contribute to someone's discovery and recovery. Food is an important marker for many of us, reflecting good and bad times, which all contribute to who we are. Helen has done an outstanding job with this book and I hope those who read it will feel the hope for the future that permeates every page.

Professor Mike Cooke CBE
Chief Executive

Food is such a comfort to so many of us; something that is vital for life and for living, but is also connected to contentment, delight and nourishment – of body and soul. The pleasure does not just come from eating, but from the preparation: selecting the menu, choosing the ingredients, preparing them – chopping, slicing, dicing, mixing and grating, kneading, seasoning and marinading ... Then there is the cooking, stirring, simmering – and all those aromas that are both tantalising and reminiscent of other meals taken in other company. The smell of warm family memories, of picnics in sunshine, or of conversations over a candlelit dinner with friends. This book brings all of this together: good memories of good times, good friends and family, and good food.

The experience of mental health problems can be so catastrophic and frightening that it shakes you to the core, obliterates memories of good times, crushes your sense of who you are, buries your belief in your own potential. It can be all consuming and overwhelming. For all of us, it is essential to find ways of moving forward, of building on our skills and strengths, recollecting and celebrating the good times, identifying hopes and dreams and having the courage to take those first small steps towards them. Although this sounds simple, it is often a huge challenge ... Memories can be painful in so many ways, hopes and dreams risk failure and disappointment, strengths and skills are hard to find when your self-confidence is at rock bottom; it is easy to understand how some people feel like giving up. But this book offers an antidote to all that anguish.

Whilst there are references to painful times, these make it all the more poignant as we find ourselves lost in brief moments of happiness, smiling as we share in memories that are brought alive by the wonderful illustrations. Before we know it we find our own hopes are kindled with dreams of creating food to share. The recipes are varied, there is something for every occasion, they are familiar rather than daunting. They tempt us towards our own future, offering a glimpse of what we might be able to do one day as we move forward in our own recovery.

Dr Julie Repper, Recovery Lead, Nottinghamshire Healthcare
Associate Professor University of Nottingham

Preface

An abiding memory for me is of standing at Grandma's gate, where the 'Blue Moon' rose bloomed, waiting for the fish man to deliver the 'yellow fish' which would be served with home-baked wholemeal bread, and vegetables from Grandad's allotment.

The smells of the rose, the smoked haddock and particularly the bread are my link to the vivid memory of sharing food at my grandparents' house. Equally the heritage of cooking as a child, alongside my mother, brings positive and lasting memories of family life, constantly rekindled through the aromas wafting out of my kitchen today.

It is this association of smell with memory which has become the focus of my second book *Nourishing: Recipes and Reflections on Recovery.* The cosmopolitan array of breads pictured on the cover symbolises the ethos of diversity and inclusivity inherent in this project. All cultures, all religions, share an interest in this staple food whose delicious smell as it bakes has the power to evoke strong memories.

Dip into this scrapbook of personal recollections and recipes pieced together from meetings with Nottinghamshire Healthcare's patients, employees, service users and carers and you will share in a story and cookery activity where barriers have been broken down and recipes have been exchanged within a mutually empowering and warm interaction, with food and families as the focus. You may recognise and identify with some of the very personal memories, values and beliefs. Your interest in home-cooked food may be stimulated. The unhealthy eating behaviours born out of our busy lives may be challenged and barriers may be broken down.

Above all, *Nourishing: Recipes and Reflections on Recovery* has already gone some way to achieving what its title promises – to supply a means of support through growth, nutrition, development and well-being – where there is a celebration of positive strategies for dealing with mental, physical and educational needs and recovery, by reducing stigma and recognising a common interest in the preparation and sharing of food.

Please embrace the essence of this project and enjoy the positive outcomes within the pages of this book.

Helen Ashwell
August 2012

"He nosed his way from smell to smell; the rough, the smooth, the dark, the golden. He went in and out, up and down, where the women sit combing their hair, where the bird-cages are piled high on the causeway, where the wine spills itself in dark red stains on the pavement, where cloth is beaten, where vine leaves tremble, where men sit and drink and spit and dice – he ran in and out, always with his nose to the ground ..."

Smell and taste are two of the traditional five senses, and as such they are an essential part of daily life. With our taste we are able to detect the flavour of food and to distinguish it from other substances that are more toxic and less palatable. Although we notice taste through taste buds in the tongue, the smell, temperature, and texture of the food we consume are also vital contributors to how we experience and register it.

Taste is important for survival, as we learn to like or dislike things according to their effect on our bodies; for instance, detecting the 'sweet' flavour helps to identify energy-rich foods, whilst bitterness serves as a warning sign for poisons. Additionally, food preferences are strongly influenced by social behaviour. We talk about 'acquired tastes' as an appreciation for a food or drink that one is liable to dislike initially, a category which includes many of the world's delicacies. Human beings need to have a varied and nutritious diet in order to live healthily; on the other hand, we are usually cautious about trying new food as it can be potentially toxic. Consequently caution towards new, potentially poisonous, substances should be balanced with our need for variety.

Research shows that infants are first exposed to the flavour of food before they have been born, as flavours are transferred from the mother to the foetus by means of the amniotic fluid periodically ingested via the unborn child's mouth and nose. Moreover, newborns are exposed to flavours through breast milk if they are breastfed[1], as for example a mother of Mediterranean extraction may expose their babies to garlic more than a British mother might.

Conversely, the impact that taste has on adults' food intake is much less apparent[2]. Adult taste preferences and aversions are not always direct indicators of food consumption, probably because of weight-related attitudes and concerns regarding anticipated consequences of food ingestion, such as how healthy or fattening food is, how easy it is to get, or how cheap or expensive it may be. Overall, an adult human pays far closer attention to fashion and social dynamics with food than babies or other mammals.

14

'Smell' is technically termed the olfactory sense. Olfactory cells in the nose are neuronal cells originating inside the brain. Both taste and olfaction are activated by chemical substances: we only need small amounts of the substances to get the part of the brain in charge of registering them stimulated. The response to a smell or taste is very fast and as with taste, the perception of smells is also linked to survival. With women, the sense of olfaction is stronger than with men, and reaches its strongest around the time of ovulation. Humans can also detect close blood-related relatives (mothers and children but not husbands and wives) via their personal scent.

We know very little of the way that smells are transmitted in the brain; however it is understood that the areas in the brain linked to memory, emotion, territorial behaviour, aggression, and sexuality are all stimulated by smells. The brain has a type of map for different odours but how this functions is not well known.

Although we detect five basic distinct flavour types with our tongue, the nose can distinguish from amongst hundreds of substances, even in minute quantities. In addition, our noses have unusual properties; for example, each nostril has separate inputs to the brain with the result that it is possible for humans to perceive different smells in each nostril simultaneously, each competing with the other.

How smells and taste can evoke past memories is still unclear. However, as mentioned above, areas stimulated by taste and smells are connected to survival, reproduction, emotions and memory. In some psychiatric conditions such as Post-Traumatic Stress Disorder, flashbacks are common, and in cases where the trauma is related to smell, olfactory flashbacks are common. Clinicians can make use of techniques such as different pleasurable smells or flavoured food as therapeutic interventions to bring the patient back into the present, often to great effect.

Dr Nuri Gene-Cos, Consultant Psychiatrist and Trauma Therapist, Lead Clinician at the Traumatic Stress Service, Maudsley Hospital, London

References

1. Gerrish C, Mennella JA. Short-term influence of breastfeeding on the infants' interaction with the environment. Developmental Psychobiology. 2000;36:40–48.
2. Birch LL, Sullivan SA. Measuring children's food preferences. Journal of School Health. 1991;61:212–214.

Epigraphs from *Flush: A Biography*, Virginia Woolf (Vintage: Chippenham, 2002).

"Where Mrs Browning saw, he smelt; where she wrote, he snuffed."

"I have felt happy and sad from the point of view that the people who made my past memories possible are no longer here with us"

"I have made great changes to my diet"

"It has been fun to recreate the smells and tastes that I remember from being a child. Thank you for the opportunity"

"It felt really good talking about food that I had as a younger person"

"I have enjoyed being part of a team"

"This was a lovely experience — uplifting, chatting and sharing stories with other people"

Thoughts and feelings
of the people involved with this project

"Cooking meals from scratch is something that I aim to do as well as is humanly and time possible"

"This project was a reminder of what was achieved and can be achieved"

"This project felt 'adult like'"

"I have really enjoyed every aspect of this project and feel that I have really benefitted from this experience. It has helped me improve my knowledge and boost my confidence and it was a nice way to recall memories from my childhood"

"It made me feel homely and reminds me of my mum"

"I would love to do this again!"

"I have really enjoyed everyone's company and felt good sharing my past stories with everyone"

17

About *Nourishing*

The key ingredients which make this book special

Recipe books exist which are linked to memoirs and personal memory, but there is a dearth of material available to link mental and physical health with stories of recovery. *Nourishing: Recipes and Reflections on Recovery* seeks to fill this gap.

For 15 months Nottinghamshire Healthcare funded me to spend half of my working week on the *Nourishing* project, of which this book is the end result. I consider it a privilege to have been involved in both.

The project involved meetings with people within the Trust who are, or have been, involved in a personal journey of recovery. My aim was to look at how memories of food sparked off and intertwined with other recollections and reflections in peoples' lives, and what impact this might have on recovery. The service users, patients, carers and staff who were my collaborators produced recipes they associated with positive memories, and which they share with you through the pages of this unique book.

For the project to take off it was vital that all those who took part felt empowered to tell their story. I felt particularly privileged to have the confidence of so many people and be entrusted with personal memories, feelings and emotions through the shared activities of storytelling and cookery.

We worked, chatted and ate together on a level playing field, where clinical conditions were put to one side and the old 'us' and 'them' barriers of staff and patient ceased to exist. From the feedback I received during the project, it became clear that this process helped some people to think about how to start taking control of their lives.

People's views are inevitably embedded in cultural heritage. One of the key aims of this book is to raise awareness about different cultures and family traditions. This project provided an opportunity to share recipes and tell stories from around the world, bringing a vibrancy of flavours and emotions. There is no doubt in my mind that the commonality of food and cooking generated wide-ranging conversations, and helped to break down barriers.

We need to break down stigma and any discriminatory barriers to give people opportunities, so that with the right support they are able to get on with their lives. My aim was to create an inclusive project which was focused on the individual journey to 'wellness' – for example, participants included patients who because of their current mental state and behavioural problems were not able to access the full range of recreational activities.

Sometimes people with mental health problems say that life happens around them and they don't feel in control; they feel bored, alienated and unconnected. One contributor had difficulty in connecting with other people. During our sessions people were able to express feelings and pleasure was taken in joining in the sharing of food. It became clear that food and family generated interest and provided the stimulus to reflect on happier times.

I worked Trust-wide, from high security to community settings, with people on a wide spectrum of need. I was able to get away from aspects of institutionalisation by getting to know the participants as individuals. They ranged from those who either remembered hopes and aspirations before becoming unwell or who are currently living and working alongside their mental health experiences.

My work went beyond the confines of mental health into the realms of physical and educational need where patients, service users, staff and carers shared a common factor: their individual need. The stories and recipes in the book come through a journey of self-discovery, where adjustments have to be made and where everyone's level of coping is different.

Ultimately, I feel that sharing, identifying and empathising with personal journeys, memories, values and beliefs can lead to personal empowerment, confidence and a sense of purpose.

About *Nourishing*

Key healthcare issues

About one in four people living in the UK experience mental health problems in any one year[1]. Even though this figure represents around a quarter of the population, society still views people with mental health problems with some trepidation and discrimination. This stigma alone can be difficult to deal with, but individuals may also be burdened with physical health problems such as obesity, type 2 diabetes and coronary heart disease, which are often linked to lifestyles and types of medication[2]. This makes the recovery journey in both mental and physical health an enormous challenge.

Mental health problems have a complex relationship with social exclusion and educational failure, and poor literacy levels are strongly associated with social exclusion[3]. At both strategic and service level, many national and local projects and interventions to improve nutrition and promote social inclusion through lifelong learning have resulted in marked reductions in mental health problems[4]. There is a need to bring together these elements in relation to mental and physical health and education, underpinned by the principles of recovery.

Obesity has become a major public health concern[5]. National statistics for the UK for 2009 show that one in four adults is currently classified as obese (BMI 30kg / m^2 or over[6]) and this figure is set to double by 2050[7]. Despite obesity being a preventable condition it is still considered to be the major cause of other diseases and disabilities, including mental health problems, coronary heart disease, some types of cancer and diabetes[8].

References

1. Department of Health, (2011), No health without mental health, Crown copyright.
2. Cormac. R, Hallford. S, Hart. L, Creasey. S and Ferriter. M, (2008), Evaluation of an Integrated Weight Management and Fitness programme in a High Secure Psychiatric Setting, Journal of The Psychiatrist, 32:95–98.
3. National Institute of Adult Continuing Education (NIACE), (2005), Learning and Skills for People Experiencing Mental Health Difficulties, Leicester, UK.
4. Repper. J and Perkins. R, (2003), Social Inclusion and Recovery: A model for Mental Health Practice, Bailliere Tindall, London.
5. National Institute for Health and Clinical Excellence, (2006), Obesity: guidance on the prevention, identification, assessment and management of overweight and obesity in adults and children, CG43.

Healthcare professionals face many challenges when devising prevention and treatment strategies for the management of overweight and obese patients. Why someone becomes obese can be difficult to determine.

The issue is extremely complex and there are no easy answers, but poor nutrition and food choices, unhealthy eating behaviours, severe mental illness, psychosocial aspects, socio-economic status and unhealthy lifestyles are often contributory factors[9].

Nourishing aims to raise awareness about home-cooked food and nutrition, by offering suggestions for balanced meals and by encouraging the reader to start looking at food in a positive way. It offers a more structured approach to mealtimes which could reduce the urge to overeat.

Despite all the complexities surrounding food and issues associated with it, I hope this book will prove to be an important resource in reducing diet-related illnesses – for instance linking to current Department of Health strategies and NHS targets for improving the quality of life for patients with mental health problems. From a clinical perspective, using forgotten food smells, tastes and past memories as a medium to engage with a patient or service user may break down some difficult barriers, and could be a measurable aspect of recovery.

6. World Health Organisation, (2006), Global Database on Body Mass Index, [online], http://apps.who.int/bmi index.jsp accessed 02.03.12.

7. Department of Health, (2010), Healthy lives, healthy people: our strategy for public health in England, Open Government Licence, Kew, London.

8. Ellis. L.J, Lang. R, Shield J.P, Wilkinson J.R, Lidstone J.S, Coulton S, and Summerbell C.D, (2006), Obesity and disability – a short review, Journal of Obesity, 7(4):341–5.

9. National Academy of Sciences, (2001), Positive Health: Resilience, Recovery, Primary Prevention, and Health Promotion, [online], http://www.ncbi.nlm.nih.gov/books/NBK43790 accessed 01.03.12.

About *Nourishing*

Who is this book for?

Nourishing was developed using a three-pronged approach to healthcare: mental health, physical health and educational needs, and aims to raise awareness by looking at ways to achieve optimum health and well-being. It aligns well with the World Health Organisation (WHO) global strategy on diet, physical activity and health, by aiming to help create environments that empower and encourage behaviour change for individuals and families, in communities and institutions.

A personal narrative is a valid way of understanding people's lives – this book can be used in therapeutic activities in a clinical setting, or with family and friends, as an impetus to kick-start independent living.

So I see this book as having something in it for everyone: from the Trust's service users, patients and employees through to the wider public and health professionals working outside the Trust.

My hope is that it will play a part in reducing stigma as well as celebrating positive strategies for dealing with mental, physical and educational needs through stories of recovery.

What's in the book?

Within the pages of *Nourishing* you will find a collection of 77 recipes, representing something very special to the people who have prepared and made them.

However, this book isn't just about the recipes, important though they are. Food smells, tastes and textures can take a person back in time and rekindle a forgotten memory, one that is individual and personal. The narratives alongside the recipes provide a snapshot of some of the reflections and memories evoked during the course of this project.

The book and font size have been designed to help people who have poor eyesight or for people who may need some support with literacy.

Book title

The book was given the name of *Nourishing* following a Trust-wide competition. The brief was for patients, service users, carers and staff to think up a title that would encapsulate the essence of the book – which is to promote inclusivity, generate interest about home-cooked food and identify and empathise with individual narratives and personal journeys of recovery.

The people behind the winning name will have their personal recipes featured on Trust-wide patients' menus.

The stories – reflections on recovery

The stories which accompany the recipes are unique and very special to the individuals who took part in the *Nourishing* project.

I feel extremely honoured to have been involved in working with people on their personal reflections of recovery in sessions where individuals were able to talk openly and freely in a safe environment.

Throughout the book you will read inspiring and compelling stories which raise awareness about personal difficulties and provide impetus for other people to take back control of their lives. You will also notice there is no differentiation between the personal reflections of patients, service users, carers and staff – we are all human, we all experience both good and bad times.

About *Nourishing*

The recipes

Most of the recipes illustrated in this book have been chosen and made by people who either use the services of Nottinghamshire Healthcare or are employed by the Trust – or both! In addition, since many of them are traditional family dishes, some people had to rely on members of their family to remember key ingredients and cooking methods so that the recipes could be replicated successfully.

The making of the recipes involved 'cook and eat' sessions in which small groups of patients, service users, carers and staff took part. With food as a focal point, these sessions proved to be a fantastic way of breaking down barriers, and helped people move away from illness and concentrate on recovery – it was an inspiring experience to observe.

Since the recipes are personal to the individuals who took part in the project, the way in which the ingredients and method are written down vary from recipe to recipe. To maintain this individuality I have been faithful to the original recipes as far as possible, just making alterations where necessary to ensure they will replicate successfully.

The recipes come from many parts of the world, so I have included a map as a visual aide-memoire to link each of them to the area understood to be their place of origin.

Most of the fruit and vegetables used in the recipes were cultivated and freshly picked from the Trust's horticulture areas and our very own farm shop at Wathwood Hospital, near Rotherham. Other ingredients were sourced locally wherever possible.

The preparation and cooking times vary from recipe to recipe – some take only 10 minutes whilst others may take between 2–3 hours.

You will see a calorific value attributed to each recipe to give you an idea of how many calories (Kcals) are in one meal portion. It is useful to know how many calories are in a meal to help you maintain a healthy weight.

In the UK the average energy (Kcals) requirements of the population vary according to age and gender:

Age	Men: Kcals per day	Women: Kcals per day
19–50 years	2550	1940
50–64 years	2380	1900
65–74 years	2330	1900
75+ years	2100	1810

(COMA report, Dietary Reference Values, 1991)

In line with current thinking on healthy eating, some pages have a healthy eating hint which gives a suggestion on how you can modify a recipe to make it even healthier.

About *Nourishing*

Illustrating the book

Front cover image

Home-made bread was chosen as the theme for the front cover of *Nourishing* for many reasons. For a start, bread is a familiar staple food providing nourishment across different cultures and religions – it is a good source of starchy carbohydrate, which can contribute towards your daily balanced diet.

But bread – especially home-made bread – is more than just a type of food. It has the ability to generate conversation and break down barriers, and you would be hard-pressed to refuse a slice when confronted with the comforting aroma of recently baked bread.

I'm a huge advocate of home-made bread and I'm thrilled by the recent re-emergence in the popularity of bread making. There is no mystery to making bread – anyone can do it, you just need a few simple ingredients, a bit of time and a lot of love! Bread making can be therapeutic and very rewarding, and something to share with friends and family.

The diverse and exquisite collection of home-made breads shown in the photograph was the result of collaboration between patients, service users, carers and staff across Nottinghamshire Healthcare. The bread making was carried out within educational and therapeutic group activities as well as on an individual basis and, as you'd expect, generated lots of discussion!

Recipes and stories

Each of the illustrations used in this book has a special significance, whether for personal or family reasons. I hope that the beautifully prepared food and photography will whet your appetite and encourage you to try out some of the recipes. Sometimes the photographs use items which hold particular memories – for example a treasured piece of handcrafted pottery made by the participant provides the serving dish for one of the recipes.

In addition, the accompanying stories have been illustrated to highlight a particular element of the story. In some cases permission was given to use non-identifiable photographs or family possessions – in one story, a photograph of personal artwork stamps a special hallmark.

As these elements come together on the page they evoke a sense of the inner person I have been privileged to get to know and can now share with you, the reader.

About *Nourishing*

Illustrating the book

The photo 'scrapbook' collection

I had a vision when first developing *Nourishing* that the look and feel of the book was one that would resemble a scrapbook: a collection of past memories, recipes and personal journeys of self-discovery that reflected the diversity of the service users, patients, carers, staff and communities within our Trust.

The 'scrapbook' section includes photographs kindly supplied by the book's contributors, as well as various images taken during the course of the project. For instance, the images of hands getting stuck into raw ingredients are actual shots taken from the activities, out of which the polished end results were born. This is graphic proof that people are not afraid of hard work!

You will also see images reflecting various community settings within the Trust, for example the horticultural areas, where patients and service users take part in therapeutic activities ranging from gardening, building and joinery to caring for animals.

The Trust's very own farm shop at Wathwood Hospital is also illustrated. This is a relatively new enterprise which has received an incredible amount of positive feedback. It provides services for patients, carers, staff and local communities and gives people in care the opportunity to gain valuable and accredited skills such as retail and customer service.

Glossary and useful stuff

The glossary is presented towards the back of the book, where there is a collection of useful information from people across the breadth of the Trust – including people not involved in providing recipes and recollections.

This is a delightful collection of bits and pieces: some of it will help you to identify certain key ingredients dotted around the book, whilst other information may help to generate an interest about different perspectives in relation to food, traditions, family and culture.

... and finally

What I have seen throughout the course of the *Nourishing* project confirms the positive outcomes that can flow from people coming together in sharing recipes and stories involving individual personal journeys, adversity, cultures, values and beliefs.

Using this book as an illustrated resource, I believe that the key objectives of this project could be applied and developed for future clinical interventions in helping patients and service users to lead more independent lives.

Healthy tips

It is very important to remember to enjoy the whole process of planning, cooking, eating and enjoying food. A good balance of food (nutrients) is vital for health and well-being.

Our contributors want to celebrate their recipes and stories with you and share their wealth of knowledge and their experiences in:

- Creating home-cooked food
- Changing the way people think about mental health problems
- Changing the way people deal with some of their mental health problems
- Dealing with some of their physical health problems
- Managing their educational needs
- Demonstrating that people can become independent and live well even on a small budget
- Showing that you can eat well, balance your diet and still eat treats in moderation
- Sharing, identifying and empathising with how people cope in times of difficulty and distress

What's so good about home-cooked food?

There are so many reasons to cook meals from scratch:

- Cooking for yourself, friends and family can be fulfilling and rewarding
- A great way of developing your time management skills, coping skills, budgeting skills
- Can be fun and really good for your self-esteem
- A more regulated way of eating, so that you know exactly what has gone into preparing your meal. For example, fewer calories, salt and saturated fat, less added sugar than takeaway or ready-made meals
- Home-cooked food is often much cheaper and can go a lot further than takeaway or ready-made meals
- Practice one of our featured recipes to impress friends or family members
- A creative way to develop vital employability skills

Tips on eating a healthy balanced diet

Eating a healthy, balanced diet is an important part of maintaining good health. Eat the right number of calories (Kcals) for how active you are, so that you balance the energy you consume with the energy you use. If you eat or drink too much, you'll put on weight. If you eat too little you'll lose weight. See page 25 for Estimated Average Requirements (EAR) for energy. Most adults eat more calories than they need, and should eat fewer.

Eat a wide range of foods to ensure that you're getting a balanced diet and that your body is receiving all the nutrients it needs.

The eatwell plate

food.gov.uk

Crown copyright. Department of Health in association with the Welsh Assembly Government, the Scottish Government and the Foods Standards Agency in Northern Ireland

Use the eatwell plate to help you get the balance right. It shows how much of what you eat should come from each food group.

The 5 food groups are:

- Green band – fruit and vegetables (33%)
  We should eat at least 5 portions a day.
- Yellow band – starchy foods (complex carbohydrates) (33%)
  We should aim to eat starchy foods at each meal time. Examples: bread, rice, potatoes, cereal, pasta
- Pink band – protein (12%)
  We should eat a moderate amount per day. Examples: fish, meat, eggs, legumes
- Blue band – milk and dairy foods (15%)
  We should eat a moderate amount per day. Examples: cheese, milk
- Purple band – foods and drinks high in fat and/or sugar (7%)
  We should eat a minimal amount per day. Examples: crisps, confectionery, cakes and fizzy drinks

Food safety tips:

— Make sure your fruit and vegetables are washed well before you use them

— Keep all work surfaces clean and tidy to prevent cross contamination and food-borne illnesses

Healthy tips

Here are eight tips to get started:

1. Base your meals on starchy foods

Starchy foods include potatoes, cereals, pasta, rice and bread. Choose wholegrain varieties when you can: they contain more fibre, and can make you feel full for longer. Try to include at least one starchy food with each main meal.

2. Eat lots of fruit and vegetables

It's recommended that we eat at least five portions of different types of fruit and vegetables a day. They are packed with vitamins, minerals and fibre, which may help reduce the risk of many diseases such as cancer and coronary heart disease. Eating five a day is easier than it sounds. A glass of 100% unsweetened fruit juice can count as one portion, and vegetables cooked into dishes also count.

3. Eat more fish

Fish is a good source of protein and contains many vitamins and minerals. Aim for at least two portions a week, including at least one portion of oily fish. Oily fish is high in omega-3 fats, which may help to prevent heart disease. Oily fish include salmon, mackerel, fresh tuna and sardines. Non-oily fish include haddock, plaice, cod, tinned tuna and hake.

4. Cut down on saturated fat and sugar

We all need some fat in our diet, but it's important to pay attention to the amount and type of fat we're eating. There are two main types of fat: saturated and unsaturated. Too much saturated fat can increase the amount of cholesterol in the blood, which increases your risk of developing heart disease. Saturated fat is found in many foods, such as hard cheese, cakes, biscuits, sausages, cream, butter, lard and pies. For a healthier choice, use just a small amount of vegetable oil or reduced fat spread instead of butter, lard or ghee.

Most people in the UK eat and drink too much sugar. Sugary foods and drinks, including alcoholic drinks, are often high in calories, and could contribute to weight gain. They can also cause tooth decay, especially if eaten between meals. Cut down on sugary fizzy drinks, alcoholic drinks, cakes, biscuits and pastries, which contain added sugars: this is the kind of sugar we should be cutting down on rather than sugars that are found naturally in foods such as fruit and milk.

5. Eat less salt

About three quarters of the salt we eat is already in the food we buy, such as shop bought soups and sauces. Eating too much salt can raise your blood pressure. People with high blood pressure are more likely to develop heart disease or have a stroke.

6. Get active and be a healthy weight

If you're trying to lose weight, aim to eat less and be more active. Eating a healthy, balanced diet will help. Aim to cut down on foods that are high in fat and sugar, and eat plenty of fruit and vegetables. Being active doesn't have to mean hours at the gym: you can find ways to fit more activity into your daily life, and being physically active may help reduce the risk of heart disease, stroke and type 2 diabetes.

7. Don't get thirsty

We need to drink about 1.2 litres of fluid every day to stop us getting dehydrated. This is in addition to the fluid we get from the food we eat. All non-alcoholic drinks count, but water, milk and fruit juices are the healthiest. Try to avoid sugary soft and fizzy drinks that are high in added sugars – they can be high in calories and bad for teeth.

8. Don't skip breakfast

Some people skip breakfast because they think it will help them lose weight. In fact, research shows that eating breakfast can help people control their weight. A healthy breakfast is an important part of a balanced diet, and provides some of the vitamins and minerals we need for good health. Wholemeal cereal, with fruit sliced over the top, is a tasty and nutritious breakfast.

These tips are based on current advice from the Food Standards Agency

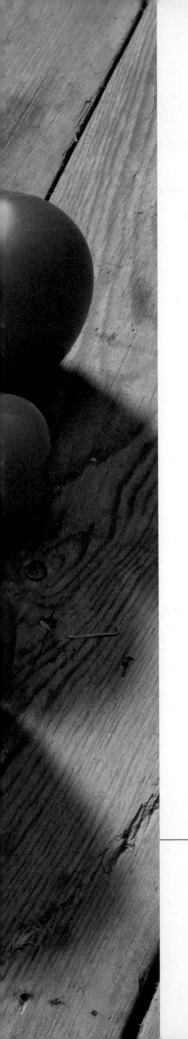

Lunch & Light Bites

Morgan's omelette

Makes 1 omelette

Ingredients

2–3 medium sized eggs (depends how hungry you are!)
A splash of semi-skimmed milk
1 small handful of mushrooms – washed, sliced thinly and lightly fried in a little olive oil
1 slice of ham – chopped
Matchbox size piece of cheese, grated – I prefer apple-smoked or mature Cheddar
Pinch of salt and pepper
A little olive oil

Method

- Crack eggs into a medium sized bowl and gently whisk, stir in the milk, salt and pepper
- Heat a deep non-stick frying pan over the hob with a little olive oil
- Pour the egg mixture into the frying pan and cook for approx 3–4 mins
- Layer the cheese, mushrooms and ham over the egg mixture, finish with cheese on top
- Transfer to the grill for approx 2–3 mins, until slightly golden in appearance and cheese has melted

My tips: Serve with mixed salad e.g. lettuce, tomatoes, cucumber and onion

Optional – serve with a small dollop of tomato ketchup

474 Kcals per omelette

> *Just over a year ago, my dad started to make this omelette as part of a healthy lifestyle. My dad's cooking inspired me to cook, so I decided to make the omelette for his tea.*
>
> *I enjoyed making it and my dad was really pleased and proud of me and said, 'Can you make me another one please!'*

Cheese scones

Makes 6 scones

Ingredients

200g / 8oz white or wholemeal self-raising flour
25g / 1oz polyunsaturated margarine
50g / 2oz mature Cheddar cheese – grated
1 teaspoon wholegrain mustard
1 small egg beaten
½ small cup semi-skimmed milk
Pinch of salt and pepper

Method

- Preheat oven to 200ºC, 400ºF, gas mark 6
- Put the flour in a bowl with a pinch of salt and pepper
- Rub in the margarine until the mixture resembles fine breadcrumbs, then add the cheese and mustard
- Mix the egg and milk together
- Add most of the egg and milk mixture to the cheese and flour bowl
- Keep stirring until it forms a soft dough
- On a clean, floured surface, roll out until thumb-sized thickness. Using a small cutter cut out and place on a baking tray
- Using a pastry brush, brush the remaining egg mixture gently on the top of each scone
- Put the scones in the oven, bake on the top shelf for about 10 mins or until they look a golden colour
- Transfer onto a cooling rack

181 Kcals per scone

> I was in a children's home when I was very young, with lots of other children.
>
> I remember eating my meals in the dining room; it was a very big room with lots and lots of tables in rows.
>
> I loved to eat cheese scones, we had them at teatime and they were cold. I sometimes had jam on them.
>
> I could look outside and there was a grass area but no flowers. The grass area had a rubber tyre swing which I loved to play on. There were lots of wooden seats for staff and children to sit on.
>
> One Christmas Matron bought me a Star Trek action man.

One of my favourite family snaps

Cullenskink

Serves 6

Ingredients

2 medium sized smoked haddock fillets – skinned and boned
1 large onion – peeled and finely chopped
6 medium sized potatoes – peeled and cut into bite-sized chunks
A large handful of fresh parsley – finely chopped
2 bay leaves
600ml / 1 pint cold water
300ml / ½ pint semi-skimmed milk
170g tin of evaporated milk
1 dessertspoon of cornflour – mixed to a paste with cold water
1 tablespoon single cream
Pinch of salt and pepper
1 tablespoon olive oil

Method

- Gently sauté the onion in a large saucepan with the olive oil until soft and translucent in appearance

- Stir in the potatoes, then add the water and semi-skimmed milk, bay leaves, parsley, salt and pepper. Simmer for 10 mins

- Meanwhile trim the smoked haddock and cut into small chunks. Place any leftover fish pieces into the saucepan to add flavour

- Now stir in the smoked haddock chunks and the evaporated milk. Simmer gently for another 15 mins – after 10 mins thicken slightly with cornflour. Stir occasionally

- Take off stove, cool slightly and remove bay leaves. Stir in the single cream

Serve with crusty bread

154 Kcals per serving (based on using light evaporated milk)

> *Cullenskink was a soup that my dad would make. My dad was a deep sea fisherman and he would often be away from home for long periods of time. While he was away cullenskink would often be made on board the boat, and the fisherman would take it in turns to make it. When my dad came home he would make the soup for the family.*
>
> *My dad was a keen cook and would often experiment with different foods and flavours. However, the recipe for cullenskink was rigid – it was handed down from previous generations. Everyone who makes cullenskink in Northern Scotland has very strong opinions as to how to make the soup, claiming to be the expert!*
>
> *My dad had an accident whilst working on the boats and became immobile. My mum took over the role of making cullenskink. My mum has recently made this dish for me – it tasted good and felt like old times.*

Rustic pea and ham soup – with a twist

Serves 6–8

Ingredients

4–5 large spuds – peeled
3 large leeks
1 swede (medium sized)
7 large carrots
1 large white onion
2 vegetable stock cubes
200g / 8oz pease pudding – homemade (see page 190) or tinned
Cold water – just enough to cover the lot in the pan
A small bacon or gammon joint (precooked or raw)

Method

- If using a raw bacon/gammon joint, preheat the oven to 160°C, 325°F, gas mark 3

- Roast the joint (20 mins per 450g / 1lb plus 20 mins over). Cool slightly. Then carve roughly. Set aside. If using a precooked joint, take out of the packaging and carve roughly. Set aside

- Peel and chop the spuds as you would do for Sunday lunch – place in a big pan or cauldron. Cover with cold water and parboil for about 5–6 mins. Drain and rinse well in cold water

- Put the drained spuds and the pease pudding back into the pan. Now add boiling water – enough to cover the spuds and the pease pudding. Stir until the pease pudding melts – over a low heat

- Chop, peel, slice, dice, cut, shred, hoy-in all the rest of the vegetables

- Crumble in the stock cubes and cover with water (as much or as little as you wish)

- Allow to simmer gently for about 30–40 mins, stirring now and again

- Now add the carved ham (as much or as little as desired). Carry on gently simmering

- When you're happy and the ingredients come together and look like a soup/broth, put into soup bowls

Serve with crusty bread

My tip: Best eaten when left to cool a bit. Can also be eaten from a plate with a knife and fork – just go easy on the water

282 Kcals per average serving

> *This recipe comes from an old miner's wife from Northumberland. It was passed down to me by my grandma, Ivy.*
>
> *It has always been one of those meals that warms you up on a cold winter's day. When I was younger, it was a treat to see Grandma cooking the soup over the stove.*
>
> *Now I have a house and family of my own, the pea and ham soup is a regular feature. I make a large batch of soup in a cauldron which will usually keep us going for at least a week.*
>
> *This soup has also got me and many a colleague through a night shift or two – it really is 'Good mood food!'*

Beefburger

Serves 2

Ingredients

2 x ¼ pounder beefburgers – home-made (see recipe below)
2 eggs – fried or poached
2 large tablespoons curried beans
2 slices white or wholemeal bread – toasted

For the beefburgers

250g / 10oz lean minced beef
25g / 1oz breadcrumbs – wholemeal
1 onion – peeled and finely chopped
1 small handful fresh parsley – finely chopped
1 egg – beaten
1 good dollop tomato ketchup
1 tablespoon olive oil
Pinch of salt and pepper

Method

- Preheat the oven to 190⁰C, 375⁰F, gas mark 5
- To make the beefburgers, gently fry the onions in a frying pan until soft, approx 5–8 mins, transfer to a sheet of kitchen paper to drain
- In a large mixing bowl put minced beef, breadcrumbs, parsley, onion, ketchup, salt and pepper. Stir in the egg, mix well
- Transfer onto a floured surface. Using your hands shape the mixture into 2 burgers
- Transfer into a frying pan, fry on both sides for 4 mins then transfer onto a baking tray and place in the oven for a further 8–10 mins (turning halfway through)
- Meanwhile fry the eggs, using a small frying pan and a little olive oil, or poach the eggs for approx 4 mins
- Heat the curried beans in a small saucepan
- Place bread in the toaster/grill to toast
- Assemble all the ingredients on two dinner plates and serve

603 Kcals per serving

> *I used to love this meal when I was a child.*
>
> *My mum would cook this for me when I came home from school when I was feeling really hungry, as dinner was usually eaten around 9 o'clock when my dad had finished work.*
>
> *When I became independent I learnt to cook this for my family.*

"I like to eat them with lots of gravy, I've always liked the taste."

Potato pattie

Makes 3 patties

Ingredients

4 medium potatoes – peeled and chopped
1 knob butter
1 splash milk
1 teaspoon sage (dried or fresh)

Crispy batter – chip shop style

1½ cups self-raising flour
1½ cups sparkling water
2 teaspoons vinegar
1 teaspoon bicarbonate of soda
Pinch of salt and pepper

Plain flour – to coat the patties

Method

- Boil potatoes for approx 20 mins until soft. Drain
- For the batter – put flour in a bowl. Make a well in the centre, gradually add the water then stir in the bicarbonate of soda, vinegar, salt and pepper
- Mash potatoes add butter, milk and sage. Cool
- Make into 3 inch (7.5 cm) diameter x 1 inch (2.5 cm) deep discs
- Coat in flour, then in the batter
- Deep or shallow fry until golden and crispy, approx 5 mins. Drain on kitchen paper

My tip: *Serve with gravy*

414 Kcals per pattie

> These patties are unique to a local area 'ull' (Hull). As a child they had a really nice taste to them, they still taste just as nice as an adult.
>
> I can remember as a child I used to get these from the local chip shop, I remember walking down the street eating the food out of a polystyrene box with my fingers. Sometimes I would have it at home with a bread bun, but I prefer it served with chips and gravy.
>
> This was a treat for me growing up, as we didn't have much money. As a teenager me and my mates from college would go to the town centre. It was a social activity for us – we would always go to the same red-coloured chip shop (Bob Carver's). This was always busy as it was in a pedestrian area full with shoppers and right next door to the local pub.

Chicken satay kebabs

Makes 2–3

Ingredients

2 tablespoons crunchy peanut butter
1 tablespoon Madras curry powder
2–3 tablespoons olive oil
1 chilli – finely chopped
1 shallot/small onion – finely chopped
2 cloves garlic – crushed, peeled and chopped
2 chicken breasts
1 teaspoon fresh ginger – peeled and grated
Medium handful rocket
2–3 pitta breads

Relish

1 large tomato or large handful baby tomatoes – finely chopped
1 small onion/1 shallot – finely chopped
1 pepper – finely chopped
½ chilli pepper – finely chopped
1 tablespoon tomato ketchup

Method

- Preheat oven to 200⁰C, 400⁰F, gas mark 6

- Place crunchy peanut butter into a bowl, followed by the curry powder, olive oil, finely chopped chilli, onion, garlic and grated ginger, mix thoroughly

- Cut chicken into strips or chunks and place into the mixture, coat well

- Either thread chicken onto skewers and put on baking tray, or place directly onto a baking tray. Put into oven for approx 25 mins, turning over halfway through until slightly golden in appearance

- For the relish – put all ingredients into a bowl, mix well

Serve in the pitta with the rocket leaves

429 Kcals per average serving

❝

Thinking about what spurred me on to cook:

- *My gran: wasn't afraid to let me cook.*
- *My dad: (a garrison butcher) let me experiment in the Army kitchen, butchery, pastry and main kitchen.*
- *Prison: where I got my City & Guilds Certificate.*

I know what I know because of a love for cooking, which each of the above contributed to in different ways.

I have worked in various places throughout my career from Military bases to OAP homes, but this recipe sticks out in my mind. Here is my story:

I went to work in a pub with full responsibilities – kitchen, menu, staff. I think my experience of à la carte cooking gave me insight. I had worked here for a while and loved the job. The landlord of the pub wanted a theme night to try and boost business after a local wine bar opened and customers dwindled. I devised a menu of Indian food – samosas, bhajis and biryani – but nothing special. I wanted to try something different – I went home and played about with some different ingredients and meats and came up with this dish: IT WAS A HIT!

❞

> I was working in a hotel, helping out in the kitchens; one of the starters on offer was garlic mushrooms (bought in). We decided to try making our own garlic mushrooms – with a difference – and this is the recipe we came up with.
>
> I enjoyed working in the hotel because I received favourable comments, I got on well with the family who owned the business and I was earning a wage too. It was a good time in my life, with happy memories.

Stuffed mushrooms

Serves 2

Ingredients

2 large field mushrooms – stalks removed
10 small button mushrooms
2 garlic cloves
1 white onion
½ cup wholemeal breadcrumbs
1 tablespoon olive oil – for cooking
Pinch of salt and pepper
Medium handful fresh flat leaf parsley and thyme – chopped
75g / 3oz goat's cheese (crumbly)
2 slices white or wholemeal bread – toasted

Method

- Preheat oven to 200^{0}C, 400^{0}F, gas mark 6
- Dice onions, crush and chop garlic and finely chop button mushrooms. Sauté the ingredients in the oil until onions are soft and the mushrooms are slightly golden
- Mix in breadcrumbs (so mixture is quite loose). Add goat's cheese, herbs, salt and pepper
- Transfer the breadcrumb mixture into centre of the large mushrooms, bake in the oven until cooked and golden brown – approx 20–25 mins
- Serve on the toast, crusts removed

377 Kcals per serving

My mum's chicken drumsticks

Serves 4

Ingredients

8 chicken drumsticks (marinated in the lemon juice for at least an hour)
1 lemon – juice

3 spring onions – finely chopped
1 clove garlic – crushed, peeled and finely chopped
½ teaspoon paprika
½ teaspoon chilli powder
1 teaspoon allspice
1 teaspoon thyme
1 teaspoon ground ginger
1 tablespoon cornflour
Pinch of salt and pepper
1 dessertspoon tomato ketchup
1 dessertspoon olive oil
Large handful fresh coriander – finely chopped

Method

- Preheat oven to 190ºC, 375ºF, gas mark 5
- Put all the ingredients (except the marinated chicken) into a large bowl and mix well
- Now add the chicken drumsticks and coat well. Marinate for a couple of hours
- Transfer onto a baking tray and put in the oven for about 30 mins – turn evenly throughout the cooking process

My tip: Serve with potato salad and green salad

155 Kcals based on 2 drumsticks

> " I've always liked spicy and well-seasoned food. I remember being about 10 years old and coming home from school and my mum cooking this meal.
>
> I often helped my mum make this meal, it brings back happy memories. "

Breads

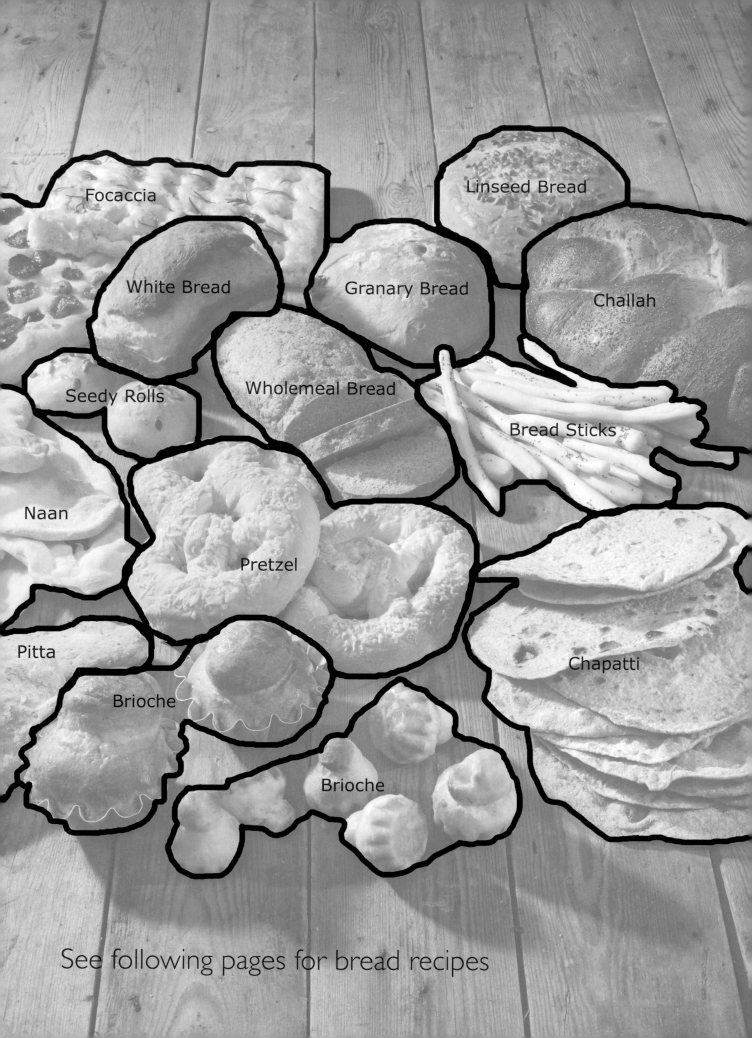

Focaccia

Linseed Bread

White Bread

Granary Bread

Challah

Seedy Rolls

Wholemeal Bread

Bread Sticks

Naan

Pretzel

Chapatti

Pitta

Brioche

Brioche

See following pages for bread recipes

This selection of bread celebrates the diversity inherent in the **Nourishing** project. Bread is a familiar staple food which provides fundamental nourishment across different cultures and religions. And, like the recipes and memories themselves, bread is for sharing.

Basic bread dough

Makes 1 large loaf, 12 bread rolls

Ingredients

3½ mugs of strong white, wholemeal or wholegrain flour (or a mixture of the three)
1½ mugs of warm kettle water
1½ teaspoons of dried yeast
1 level teaspoon of salt
1 level teaspoon of sugar
1 tablespoon of olive oil

Method

- Place the flour in a large mixing bowl. Add the salt, sugar and dried yeast and mix thoroughly

- Make a well in the centre of the flour mixture and pour in the water and olive oil. Now start bringing the dry ingredients into the wet ingredients until they form a soft dough

- Transfer the dough onto a lightly floured work surface and knead the dough by pulling the outside edges into the centre. Do this for approx 5 mins, or longer if you have time, until it becomes less sticky and feels firm to touch

- Place the dough back into the bowl and leave in a warm place until it doubles in size (this is called proving). This might take up to 1½ hours

- Now place back onto a lightly floured surface and knead again for a couple of minutes – you might start to see pockets of air (this is a good sign that the finished bread will be light and of a good texture)

- **To make the loaf:** place the dough into the prepared loaf tin, or alternatively mould into a shape of your choice, and leave in a warm place – covered with a clean tea towel until it doubles in size again – approx 30–40 mins

- **To make the bread rolls:** cut the dough into 12 portions. Using your hands shape into rounds and place onto a lightly greased baking tray. Cover with a clean tea towel and leave in a warm place until they double in size – approx 30 mins

- Place in the oven and bake the loaf for about 30 mins and the bread rolls for about 20 mins – to check they are cooked, carefully tap the bottom of the bread – if it sounds hollow it will be cooked

- Transfer onto a wire rack and leave to cool

141 Kcals per average slice/bread roll

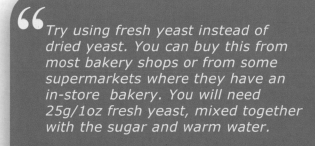

> *Try using fresh yeast instead of dried yeast. You can buy this from most bakery shops or from some supermarkets where they have an in-store bakery. You will need 25g/1oz fresh yeast, mixed together with the sugar and warm water.*
>
> *Bread making may look a little daunting, but once you start you realise that it isn't that complicated and it can be a very therapeutic and rewarding activity.*
>
> *This is a basic bread recipe – once you have mastered this you can start experimenting by adding different ingredients such as sundried tomatoes, green or/and black olives, fresh herbs – rosemary, chives etc. The possibilities are endless!*

To reduce the calorie content per slice of bread, cut thinner slices

Bread sticks – gluten free

Makes approx 15

Ingredients

125g / 5oz gluten free white bread flour
½ teaspoon dried yeast
Pinch of sugar
Pinch of salt
75ml / 2½fl oz water
1 tablespoon olive oil
2 tablespoons poppy seeds

Method

- Preheat oven to 200⁰C, 400⁰F, gas mark 6
- Mix together the flour, yeast, sugar, salt, water and oil to form a dough
- Transfer onto a floured work surface and knead for approx 5 mins
- Leave to prove in a bowl covered with a tea towel until dough has doubled in size
- Transfer dough onto a floured surface and knock back
- Divide the dough into approx 15 pieces, and roll each one into a long sausage shape
- Transfer onto a greased baking tray and sprinkle with the poppy seeds
- Allow to rise for approx 20–25 mins
- Bake for approx 10–15 mins depending on the thickness of the bread sticks
- Transfer onto a cooling rack

38 Kcals per bread stick

Brioche

Makes 12 mini brioches or 1 large one

Ingredients

3½ mugs of strong bread flour
1 teaspoon dried yeast
Pinch of salt
1 lemon or orange – finely grated for the zest
50g / 2oz sugar
50g / 2oz butter
½ mug semi-skimmed milk
3 eggs – beaten

For egg wash
1 egg – beaten

Method

- Preheat oven to 220°C, 425°F, gas mark 7
- Lightly grease the brioche tin(s)
- Place the flour in a medium sized bowl, stir in the salt, orange or lemon zest and yeast
- Place the milk and butter in a pan and warm gently until the butter has melted
- Make a well in the middle of the flour and gradually add the warm milk and butter. Mix until a soft dough has formed
- Transfer onto a lightly floured surface and knead, bringing the outside edges into the centre of the dough, do this for about 5 mins
- Place the dough back into the mixing bowl, using a clean tea towel cover and leave in a warm place until doubled in size – this can take up to 1½ hours
- Transfer dough onto a lightly floured work surface and knead again for a couple of minutes
- Cut into 13 portions; shape 12 of them into rounds then put into the prepared brioche tins and place on a baking tray. Using the remaining dough cut into 12 and again shape into 12 rounds. Using your thumb, make an indentation in each brioche and carefully place the smaller dough portion on the top
- Alternatively shape the dough into 1 large round and place into the large prepared brioche tin
- Now carefully brush the brioche top(s) with the prepared egg wash
- Leave in a warm place and cover with a clean tea towel until doubled in size – approx 30–40 mins
- Place in the oven – approx 20 mins for the mini brioches and approx 30 mins for the larger one
- Take out of oven and place on a cooling rack. Cool slightly then carefully take out of tins

210 Kcals per average slice/mini brioche

Challah

This is a traditional bread made for the Jewish Sabbath. As such the quantities in this this recipe make two loaves for up to 30 people

Ingredients

600ml / 1pt warm water
2 x 7g sachets of dried active baking yeast
7 tablespoons honey
4 tablespoons vegetable oil
3 eggs
1 tablespoon of salt
1kg / 2lb 3oz plain flour
1 tablespoon poppy seeds

Method

- Preheat the oven to 190°C, 375°F, gas mark 5

- Pour the water into a large mixing bowl, add the yeast and then beat in the honey, oil, two eggs and salt

- Then add the flour in small amounts, beating after each addition, and then as the dough thickens, knead with your hands. The mixture must be kneaded until it is smooth, with a slight shine to it and no longer sticky, adding flour as needed

- The dough should then be covered by a clean, slightly damp cloth (I use a tea towel), and left to rise for at least 1½ hours – the dough should double in size

- The dough should have the 'rise' knocked out, and then be turned out onto a floured surface and divided into half. Each half should then be kneaded for 5 mins or so, sprinkling with flour when necessary to keep it from getting sticky

- Each piece now needs to be divided into thirds and each rolled into long snakes about 4 cm /1½ ins in diameter. Pinch the ends of the three snakes together and plait from the middle

- Grease or flour 2 large baking trays and place a finished plait on each, cover with the towel again and leave to rise for an hour

- After the second rising, beat the remaining egg and brush the egg wash over both loaves, scatter with poppy seeds and place in the preheated oven for 40 minutes

- Remove from the oven and place on cooling racks

My tip: *A local honey from Leicestershire, purchased at Café Art in Trust Headquarters, is excellent*

174 Kcals per average slice

Chapatti

Makes 10

Ingredients

5 mugs wholemeal flour or medium grade 2 chapatti flour
Pinch of salt
Cold water to mix

Method

- Put flour and salt into bowl, stir in enough water to make soft dough
- Take out of bowl and knead for approx 8 mins
- Cut into 10 pieces and shape into balls
- Using a rolling pin, roll out into thin rounds on a floured work surface
- Pick up the rounds and, using both hands, gently flip from one hand to the other
- Carefully place a round of dough in a hot tawa and cook 2 mins on either side – it will look slightly golden in appearance. Continue this process with the rest of the shaped dough balls
- Transfer onto a cooling rack

138 Kcals per chapatti

Linseed bread

Makes 2 small loaves or 12 bread cakes

Ingredients

3½ mugs of strong flour – white, wholemeal or granary
2 tablespoons linseed oil
Pinch of salt
Pinch of sugar
2½ tablespoons of linseeds or mixed seeds
1 mug warm milk
½ mug warm water (from the kettle)
25g / 1oz fresh yeast
1 egg – beaten with a little milk

Method

- Preheat the oven to 200°C, 400°F, gas mark 6

- Mix the yeast and warm milk and water together in a bowl

- In a large bowl put the flour, 2 tablespoons of seeds, salt and sugar, and mix

- Make a well in the middle of the dry ingredients and add the milk, water and oil – mix well

- Transfer to a floured surface and start to knead the dough by stretching and pulling – you can be quite rough at this stage

- Place the dough back into the bowl. Cover with a tea towel and leave to prove for about 1 hour – until it doubles in size

- After an hour place the dough back onto a floured surface and knead again for a couple of minutes. Then either cut into 2 to make 2 loaves, or cut into 12 to make bread cakes

- Shape into the desired loaf or bread cake, brush with the beaten egg, and sprinkle the remaining ½ tablespoon seeds over the top

- Prove again for about 30 mins

- Transfer into the oven for approx 20 mins for bread cakes and 30 mins for loaves. Tap the underside of the bread – if it sounds hollow it will be done

- Transfer onto a cooling rack

132 Kcals per average slice/bread cake

> *I think that there is nothing nicer than the smell of fresh bread baking in the oven. This lovely smell reminds me of staying at my grandma's house.*
>
> *When I was about eight years old I remember my curiosity when watching my grandma bake, especially when she made bread. Grandma had strict rules when bread making and no one would dare to uncover and look at the dough whilst it was proving, because Grandma said it would spoil the quality of the finished loaf.*
>
> *My grandma spent a lot of time in her kitchen and my grandad spent a lot of time in the garden – he grew flowers such as gladioli – which were my grandma's favourite – and dahlias, which Grandma didn't like – she said they were full of earwigs!*

Artisan bread

Makes 1 large loaf

Ingredients

400g / 1lb strong white flour (you will find this in any supermarket in the baking section)
200g / 8oz strong wholemeal flour (this will be in the same place!)
1 x 7g sachet of dried active yeast (also the same place)
Pinch of salt – probably no more than ½ a teaspoon
1 tablespoon of sugar – and don't overdo it as the bread should not be too sweet
425ml / ¾ pint warm water

Method

- First mix all the dry ingredients together in a bowl thoroughly, and then add the warm water. You will need to mix this with a (preferably wooden) spoon first until the mixture starts to bind together roughly

- Once you have bound the ingredients together, tip the whole lot out on a floured surface and start to knead into a single ball of dough. At this stage the mixture will be sticky in some places, and dry in others. Keep kneading until it has a consistent feel – you may have to occasionally dust with flour (use the strong white) but do not use too much as this will dry the dough and it will not rise well

- The purpose of kneading the dough is to make sure the ingredients are thoroughly mixed, and also to stretch the gluten content in order that it engages with the yeast and creates the rise that is necessary

- There is a minimum time for kneading of no less than 5–6 minutes, but the more you do it, the better the rise and the taste of the finished loaf. I would recommend 10 minutes – and you will be surprised how quickly your arm muscles develop

- When the gluten has really engaged you will notice a slight shine to the dough, as if it has had a couple of drops of vegetable oil wiped over it. At that point you have done enough!

- Put the dough back in the mixing bowl and cover with a cloth – I use a clean drying-up cloth – and let it stand for 1½ hours in a warm – not hot – place. The dough should have risen quite a lot, probably doubling in size. If it has risen less than that it may be because the dough mix was too dry, or because it was not kneaded enough. That's OK, you will still get a loaf to eat at the end and you are perfecting a technique to create your own style of loaf so you will have an idea of how to make it better next time!

- Turn on the oven at this stage, as it must be hot when you put the bread in, so gas mark 7, 220°C, 425°F

- Tip the mix out of the bowl onto a lightly floured surface and gently knead again to 'knock' the air out of the dough – this time the kneading should only be very brief. The dough can then be shaped into a loaf and put on a baking tray or into a 2lb (900g) loaf tin if you have one. If you are going to bake it in a tin, the sides should be wiped with vegetable oil to make sure the loaf will come out

- The tin or tray should then be placed back into the warm place for a further 30–45 minutes for it to rise again. It should not be left for longer as the dough can collapse if left too long

- And so now put the bread into the oven for 40 minutes, and sit back and enjoy the really wonderful smell that starts to come fill the kitchen – fresh bread and all my own work! After 40 minutes take it out of the oven

- Take the loaf off the tray or out of the tin and put on a baking rack – I used the rack out of the grill pan when I started – to cool down. The reason for doing this is that if it is put on a solid surface the bottom of the loaf gets damp with condensation and can spoil the work you've done. After about an hour it will have settled and you can have your favourite bread sandwich

151 Kcals per average slice

"Congratulations, you are now a baker of bread!"

> ❝
> *I got into making bread because a friend did it, and she suggested it would be a really good way of getting all my pent-up stresses from the working day out productively. Kneading dough for 10 minutes to produce its elasticity and to get a good rising loaf is a physical thing that can bring out a sweat and definitely gets rid of my stress and anger.*
>
> *So I started making bread 35 years ago and have done it ever since as part of my own wellness plan, which also includes putting good wholesome food on the table at home.*
>
> *This is the recipe of the first loaf I made and perfected my technique from. It's really simple and as long as you follow it through you'll get a great loaf every time! This quantity will make one loaf.* ❞

Focaccia

Makes 12–15

Ingredients

3½ mugs strong bread flour
1 heaped teaspoon dried yeast
1½ mugs warm water
Pinch of salt
Pinch of sugar
1 tablespoon olive oil

Topping suggestions

A drizzle of olive oil
Fresh rosemary – roughly chopped
Garlic cloves – crushed, peeled and chopped
Green and black olives – pitted and roughly chopped
Sundried tomatoes – roughly chopped

Method

- Preheat oven to 220°C, 425°F, gas mark 7

- Lightly grease a baking tray – approx 30x15 cm (12x6 in)

- Place the flour into a large mixing bowl, add the salt, sugar and yeast and mix well

- Make a well in the centre of the flour and add the water and olive oil, mix until a soft dough is formed

- Transfer onto a lightly floured work surface and knead by bringing the outer edges into the centre of the dough. Do this for approx 5 mins until the dough becomes firm to the touch

- Place the dough back into the bowl, cover with a clean tea towel and leave in a warm place until it doubles in size – this can take up to 1½ hours

- Transfer the dough onto a lightly floured work surface and knead again for about 2 mins

- Using a rolling pin, roll the dough to fit the baking tray. Place in the tray, making sure to push the dough into the corners. Cover with a clean tea towel and leave to double in size in a warm place – approx 30–40 mins

- Using your thumb or forefinger, prod the dough to make even dimples. Now decorate with your chosen toppings and drizzle sparingly with olive oil

- Place in the oven for about 20–25 mins

- Transfer onto a cooling rack. When cool, cut into 12 squares

My tip: *To make the finished product extra soft, place a deep-sided baking tray filled with water on the shelf below the focaccia during the baking process*

116 Kcals per average serving

Naan

Makes 4–5 naans

Ingredients

250g / 8oz plain flour
½ level teaspoon baking powder
1 level teaspoon dried yeast
Pinch of sugar
Pinch of salt
150ml / 5fl oz semi-skimmed milk
1 small egg – lightly beaten and mixed with the milk
1 dessertspoon vegetable oil

Method

- Preheat the oven to 220°C, 425°F, gas mark 7
- Place the flour in a medium sized bowl, add the baking powder, salt, sugar and dried yeast – mix well
- Next, stir in the egg and milk then stir in the vegetable oil. Mix until it becomes a soft dough – you might not need all the milk
- Transfer onto a lightly floured work surface and knead by bringing the outer edges into the centre of the dough, do this for approx 5 mins until firm to touch and not sticky
- Put the dough back into the bowl and cover with a clean tea towel. Leave in a warm place until doubled in size – this can take up to 1½ hours
- Transfer back onto a lightly floured work surface and knead again for a couple of minutes then cut evenly into 4–5 portions. Using your hands, shape into rounds then, using a rolling pin, roll into a teardrop shape, about 1 inch thick
- Place onto a lightly greased baking tray and put into the oven for approx 5–6 mins until well risen
- Transfer onto a cooling rack and leave to cool slightly before serving

223 Kcals per naan (based on 5 naans)

Pitta

Makes 6–8 pittas

Ingredients

3 mugs of strong bread flour – white or wholemeal or combination of both
1 level teaspoon dried yeast
½ teaspoon salt
Pinch of sugar
½ mug of warm water
1 tablespoon olive oil

Method

- Preheat oven to 220°C, 425°F, gas mark 7
- Place the flour in a medium sized mixing bowl. Add the yeast, sugar and salt and mix well
- Make a well in the centre and add the water and olive oil. Mix until a dough is formed
- Transfer onto a lightly floured work surface and knead by bringing the edges into the middle of the dough – do this for 5 mins until the dough becomes firm and not as sticky
- Place back into the bowl, cover with a clean tea towel and leave to double in size in a warm place – this may take up to 1½ hours
- Transfer back onto a lightly floured work surface and knead again for a couple of minutes. Cut into 5–6 portions, using your hands shape into rounds then using a rolling pin, roll out into 5–6 inch (12-15 cm) lengths
- Place onto a lightly greased baking tray and put in the oven for approx 4 mins on either side
- Transfer onto a cooling rack

137 Kcals per average pitta

Pretzel

Makes 8–10 pretzels

Ingredients

500g / 1lb strong white flour
1 teaspoon salt
1 teaspoon caster sugar
1 x 7g sachet fast action dried yeast
Approx 300ml / 10fl oz lukewarm water
75g / 3oz cheddar cheese, grated

Method

- Preheat oven to 230°C, 450°F, gas mark 8
- Put flour into a large mixing bowl and stir in salt, sugar and dried yeast
- Make a well in the centre of the flour; gradually stir in the water to form a soft dough – you might need a bit more or less water
- Knead the dough on a floured surface for approx 5 mins, then put it back in the bowl, cover and leave to rise in a warm place until doubled in size (approx 30 mins)
- Put the dough back onto a floured surface and 'knock back'. Then flatten the dough with your hands and sprinkle half the cheese over the surface. Knead lightly to mix the cheese into the dough
- Divide the dough into 8 pieces
- Using your hands, roll/stretch each piece into a 'sausage' shape about 40 cm/15 in long
- Bend each shape into a crescent, bring the ends back to the centre of the crescent and make into a loose knot
- Sprinkle the rest of the cheese over the top of the pretzels and place them onto two lightly greased baking trays, leaving space between them. Cover and leave to rise in a warm place for 30 mins until they have doubled in size
- Bake for approx 15–20 mins, take out of the oven and cool on a wire rack

My tips:
— Add a handful of seeds (e.g. sesame, sunflower, pumpkin) to the flour mixture
— Replace the cheddar cheese with another hard cheese, e.g. parmesan or goat's cheese, or try a mixture
— Add some chopped olives to the dough with the cheese
— Try sweet pretzels: knead some ground cinnamon, sugar and raisins into the dough. Brush the tops of the pretzels with milk and sprinkle with cinnamon
— Cooked pretzels freeze well

197 Kcals per average pretzel

Mains

> I have been preparing this meal for my family for well over 20 years. It's one of those meals that always looks very colourful and appetising.
>
> I have recently undergone treatment for cancer; this meal has helped me during certain difficult times. When I eat it, I feel like the food is nourishing my body.
>
> I have always been a fit and active person. When I was told that I had cancer it took me a short period of time to accept it. After that I tackled it with sheer determination and optimism, and the support from my family and friends has been wonderful.

Fresh salmon and mixed vegetables

Serves 2

Ingredients

2 salmon fillets (I prefer tail end – less bones!)

1 large handful broccoli spears
1 large carrot – peeled and cut into medium slices
1 large courgette – cut into medium slices
1 large handful garden peas (fresh or frozen)

Method

To prepare the salmon

- Cover a dinner plate with cling film
- Place the prepared salmon onto the plate
- Cover the salmon with more cling film
- Place in a microwave for between 3–4 mins, depending on the microwave wattage (mine is 840W)

To prepare the vegetables

- Place the carrots in a medium sized saucepan and cover with cold water, bring to the boil
- Add peas, broccoli and courgette, boil for 5–8 mins, so still retaining a slight crunch
- Drain and serve

My tip: *Serve with boiled new potatoes*

269 Kcals per serving

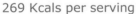

Saag aloo: potato and spinach curry

Serves 4–6

Ingredients

4 medium waxy potatoes e.g. Charlotte – washed, roughly cubed and
parboiled (boiled for approx 8 mins), drained (keep the water)
1 cup of reserved potato water
2–3 packs washed and prepared spinach
2 handfuls curry leaves – roughly chopped
1 large white onion – finely chopped
2 cloves garlic – crushed, peeled and finely chopped
Large bunch fresh coriander – roughly chopped
1 dessertspoon cumin seeds
1 teaspoon crushed or milled black peppercorns
1 heaped teaspoon turmeric
½ teaspoon cayenne pepper
1 tablespoon rapeseed oil
Pinch of salt

Method

- Place the onion and oil in a medium sized saucepan on a medium heat
  until soft – approx 4 mins. Add the garlic, curry leaves and coriander, stir
- Stir in the rest of the spices for approx 3 mins
- Add the potatoes, pinch of salt and potato water, cook for 5–10 mins,
  stirring occasionally
- Stir in the spinach, a handful at a time until slightly wilted

My tips:
- By crushing fresh coriander you release more flavour!
- This is a delicious dry curry which can be eaten on its own or
  with naan bread

125 Kcals per average serving

> When I was eight years old I was run over by a car. After getting over this
> traumatic experience, one of the noticeable differences was that I had lost
> my appetite and most types of food made me feel sick most of the time.
>
> My grandmother was originally from India, her food was different. I was
> able to eat her meals – they were very comforting and tasty – she made
> the most perfect garam masala rice, but the potato and spinach recipe (my
> grandmother also made this with chicken) has stayed with me all my life. I
> have family of my own now and they also love saag aloo.
>
> When I move on and see my children again I want to cook this meal for
> them – I also want to make spinach and poached egg with soured cream
> sauce/dip. ”

Corned beef hash

"At home we called this dish Panackelty — a dish of meat and root vegetables, historically popular with mining and shipyard families. This recipe was handed down from my mother. When I was a child we often ate this because it was cheap to make and would fill us up. Nowadays I add extra vegetables to make it a healthier meal."

Serves 4

Ingredients

6–8 medium potatoes – peeled and sliced thickly
1 large tin corned beef – medium slices
2 large onions – roughly sliced
2 large carrots peeled and roughly chopped
Gravy granules – 3 dessertspoons – 1 dessertspoon mixed with cold water to make a paste
Cold water to cover
Pinch of salt and pepper

Method

282 Kcals per serving

- Preheat oven to 200°C, 400°F, gas mark 6
- Layer the ingredients in a deep roasting tin. Start with potato, followed by onion, carrot and corned beef. Do this twice and finish off with a layer of potato
- Sprinkle with gravy granules and pour on water to cover the ingredients
- Cover with lid or tin foil
- Bake for approx 1½ hours or until potatoes are soft (stirring occasionally)
- Take out of oven and thicken slightly with the gravy granule paste

Serve with vegetables and crusty bread

My Story

When I became a mother I had already acquired the skills from my own mother to make basic wholesome meals from scratch. I picked up my cookery skills by watching what my mother did. Then gradually I became confident to cook on my own. I had to rely on this visual process because I couldn't read recipes.

I have been able to get by for years without being able to read and write much. On a day to day basis I was still able to function well, providing wholesome meals all based on memory and experimentation.

The corned beef hash was simple for me to make because there were only four key ingredients. It is a special recipe to me because it draws together two aspects of my life. It is a reminder of happy times learning to cook with my mother but it also highlights my past difficulties.

I have worked for the NHS for over 15 years. The work I have undertaken has meant I was able to keep my poor reading and writing skills a secret, although the art of keeping it a secret proved very stressful at times.

A few years ago I decided I had had enough of getting by and wanted to get some help to learn to read. As a child I had been told I was 'thick'. This stigma made me try so hard to keep up in the classroom at school but I was unable to do so.

All through my life I felt I had a 'thick' label until I decided to get help. Tests have highlighted that I have dyslexia and dyspraxia.

My Story continues overleaf

I have now been on courses to help me and have found staff involved extremely supportive. I get very frustrated that I often make the same mistakes with spellings or grammar over and over again. When I read, the lines get mixed up. They float about and this is why it takes me a long time to read a sentence. My reading and writing have improved now that I use pink or cream paper, a larger font size and have more space between letters; some people find other colours of paper help them.

People take it for granted that you can read and write. It's been less stressful now I have shared my difficulties with my work colleagues and with my managers, most of whom have been supportive. For a very long time I was worried that I would be sacked if my managers knew I had these problems.

I have been on a very long learning journey.

When I was assessed I was told that I would improve, but would probably never be able to read a book. It is a joy to me that I have proven them wrong, and now I have read a variety of books. These have been shortened forms of novels but gradually I am building the skills to enable me to read an unabridged story.

I've always enjoyed cooking for family and friends, and especially now that my repertoire has increased as my reading and writing skills have improved. I am able to read certain recipes as long as the writing is not too squashed together.

I used to be frightened to join in social events where activities might involve reading, writing or general knowledge, so I would turn down such invitations and make up excuses not to attend. Now I feel more confident and able to join in with support. My social life has improved considerably and is much more enjoyable and less stressful.

Fish en croute

"As I became more confident with my reading and writing skills. I was able to start cooking more complex dishes, which enabled me to adapt the recipes to my taste. This recipe has become a favourite in my family; my children are grown up and have left home now but will often request this when they come to visit."

Serves 4

Ingredients

4 pieces cod loin – filleted, boned and skinned
1 packet shop bought puff pastry
1 onion – finely chopped
Mushrooms – large handful, sliced
50g / 2oz smooth liver pâté
1–2 tablespoons low fat crème fraiche
1 egg – beaten
Pinch of salt and pepper

My tip: Any fish can be used

Method

- Preheat oven to 200⁰C, 400⁰F, gas mark 6

- Take the puff pastry out of the packet and let it rest for 20 mins. Cut into 2 equal pieces then roll out the first piece on a floured surface – enough to position 2 of the 4 fish fillets side by side

- Sauté the onions and mushrooms for 5 mins until soft, then cool

- In a small bowl, mix the pâté with the crème fraiche until smooth and loose in consistency

- Wash and dry the fish with kitchen roll and place two pieces in the middle of the rolled out pastry – side by side

- Next place the mushrooms and onions over the top

- Spoon over the pâté mixture

- Finish with the remaining two pieces of fish

- Roll out the second piece of pastry, slightly bigger than the first piece, and cover the rest of the ingredients. Neatly trim and crimp the edges with your fingers. Place on baking tray

- Brush with the beaten egg then put in the oven on the top shelf for approx 25–30 mins

Serve with mixed leaf salad

535 Kcals per slice

Cottage pie

Serves 4–6

Ingredients

500g / 1lb 2oz lean minced beef
1 large onion – peeled and finely chopped
2 large carrots – diced
1 cupful frozen peas
1 small tin sweetcorn
1 400g tin of plum tomatoes
1 beef stock cube, diluted in 1 pint boiling water
1 tablespoon cornflour – mixed to a paste with cold water
1 tablespoon olive oil
Pinch of salt and pepper

For the topping

2kg / 4lb potatoes – peeled and roughly chopped
1 knob of butter or sunflower margarine
A splash of semi-skimmed milk

Method

- Preheat the oven to 180°C, 350°F, gas mark 4

- Gently fry the onion in the olive oil in a large saucepan for 5–8 mins until soft. Add the carrots and stir

- Stir in the minced beef and cook until brown – 6 mins

- Next stir in the peas and sweetcorn then add the tinned tomatoes

- Add the stock, salt and pepper. Simmer for approximately 40 mins. Add more stock if necessary

- Thicken the mixture with the cornflour

- Meanwhile place the potatoes into a medium sized saucepan, cover with cold water and boil for approximately 20–25 mins until soft

- Drain the potatoes, then using a potato masher, mash with the butter and milk until smooth and lump free

- Drain the meat from most of the gravy, put meat into an ovenproof dish then carefully arrange the mashed potato over the top. Save the gravy to serve

- Transfer to the oven for about 30–40 mins until the potato is golden in colour

Serve with cabbage, roasted butternut squash and the reserved gravy

410 Kcals per average serving

82

I had been in and out of hospital a few times. As I made progress I moved into a rehabilitation unit.

Making and eating cottage pie takes me back to a time in my life where I started to rebuild my life and make improvements in my self-confidence, after losing my job and after feeling so unwell.

I remember making cottage pie for some of the people in the unit who were going through some difficult times and not looking after themselves nutritionally. I enjoyed providing others with a wholesome meal and they said that they really appreciated my kind gesture. This meal formed the basis of a continued friendship.

I am now moving further forward and will be attending full-time education. I feel very positive about the future.

"

My tip: For extra appeal add sliced tomato before putting in the oven

The Italian meal

Meat and vegetarian options

Serves 4–6

Ingredients

1 medium onion – peeled and roughly chopped
2 cloves of garlic (optional) – crushed, peeled and chopped
500g / 1lb 2oz minced pork or quorn
200g / 8oz mushrooms – sliced
1 red pepper – chopped
2 sticks of celery – finely sliced
2 heaped teaspoons tomato purée
Black pepper to season
1 chicken stock cube
150ml / ¼ pint apple juice or water
100g / 4oz mature cheddar chopped

Method

- Fry the onion and garlic in a small amount of olive oil for approximately 7 mins until soft, stirring occasionally
- Add the pork or quorn, stir for 8 mins, then drain off excess liquid
- Stir in the mushrooms, red pepper and celery, cook until tender for approximately 8–10 mins
- Stir in the tomato purée
- Sprinkle in the stock cube
- Stir in the apple juice or water
- Add pinch of salt and pepper
- Simmer for approximately 30–45 mins
- Now stir in the cheese so it melts

Serve with tagliatelle pasta – cook as per instructions on the back of the packet

My tip: This dish is suitable for freezing. I often double the quantity in order to freeze some

586 Kcals per average serving

> In the 1980s I worked for the Civil Service, in their Training Services Agency. Once a week I was invited for lunch, on a voluntary basis, by a women's support cookery group. I remember how enjoyable this was – we all sat round a large table and the atmosphere was friendly with lots of banter!
>
> I particularly remember eating and enjoying sausage meat with tomato sauce. Over the years I have adapted this meal, which has become a family favourite with my mother and my daughter – who has just become a mother herself and is appreciating the Italian meal as a food parcel from me.
>
> My family and friends seem to enjoy this meal because it is so flavoursome. It is great for dinner parties and is ideal to freeze.

Mushroom pizza

Makes 2–3 pizzas

Ingredients

250g / 10oz strong white flour
½ teaspoon of dried yeast
Pinch of salt
Pinch of sugar
150ml / 5fl oz of warm water
1 tablespoon olive oil

Tomato sauce

2 shallots or 1 small onion
1 clove garlic
2 large handfuls of cherry tomatoes
Small handful basil
Pinch of salt

Topping

1 large handful mushrooms, washed and finely sliced
Mozzarella – 1 matchbox size, cubed

Method

- Preheat the oven to 220⁰C, 425⁰F, gas mark 7

For the dough

- In a small bowl mix the warm water with the yeast and sugar. Stir in the olive oil
- Using a larger bowl, put in the flour and pinch of salt
- Make a well in the flour, add the yeast mixture and mix to form a dough (you may not need all of the liquid)
- Take the dough out of the bowl and knead on a floured surface
- Put back into the bowl, cover and rest for 30 mins

For the tomato sauce

- Finely chop the shallots/onion and crush, peel and chop the garlic
- Lightly fry in a medium sized saucepan in a little olive oil
- Add the tomatoes, pinch of salt and basil leaves
- Simmer for 15 mins, then purée in a blender and leave to cool

- Roll out the dough thinly to the size of a large side plate. Transfer onto a lightly greased baking tray
- Put 2 tablespoons of the tomato sauce over the dough, taking care not to spill over the edges (leave about 2 cm/½ in gap)
- Arrange the mushrooms and mozzarella on top. Put into oven for approx 8 mins

> 66
> *This recipe brings back memories of going to education sessions in the hospital where I am staying.*
>
> *This was the first time I had cooked and eaten pizza. There was me and another patient; it was a happy feeling and experience that I would like to feel again when I make mushroom pizza for the second time.* 99

512 Kcals per pizza (based on making 2 pizzas)

Bacon, liver and onions in tomato sauce

Serves 2–3

Ingredients

450g / 1lb liver
2 medium onions
4 rashers bacon
1 400g tin of your preferred tomato soup
2 tablespoons olive oil
A little plain flour – for dusting

Method

- Chop the onions and add to a large frying pan or wok with the olive oil
- Soften the onions on a low heat
- With kitchen scissors cut the bacon into 25mm/1 inch squares. Add to the onions, increase the heat slightly and brown slightly
- Wash the liver and pat dry with kitchen roll. Again with kitchen scissors, cut into 25mm/1 inch chunks
- Dust the liver evenly with the flour and add to the pan
- Keep turning until liver is browned all over
- Pour over the tomato soup and stir well
- Reduce the heat and simmer gently for 15–20 mins. Stir frequently

My tip: Serve with mashed potato and sliced green beans – my personal favourite choice

423 Kcals per average serving

88

My Story

When we got married my husband took on the role of cooking, something he hadn't done before. His mum gave him this recipe which over the years has become a favourite meal. Mum now has dementia and so the recipe is even more special. Apart from working as a health professional for the NHS I am now a carer for my husband who has developed type 2 diabetes. When I initially found out about his diagnosis I was shocked and thought, "I'm a health professional, why didn't I realise, and what do we do now!" Since developing diabetes my husband has smaller portions, has increased his vegetable consumption, eats wholegrain starchy food and buys low salt and sugar tomato soup for the recipe.

Tuna pasta bake

Serves 2

Ingredients

2 medium sized tuna steaks
1 medium sized onion – peeled and finely chopped
1 red pepper – deseeded and finely chopped
2 cups pasta – white or wholemeal – cooked to manufacturer's recommendations
(usually 8–10 mins)
50g / 2oz mature cheddar cheese – grated
1 tablespoon olive oil
1 small handful fresh chopped herbs e.g. parsley

For white sauce

25g / 1oz sunflower margarine
25g / 1oz plain flour
300ml / ½ pint semi-skimmed milk
1 teaspoon mustard
Pinch of salt and pepper

Method

- Preheat the oven to 200°C, 400°F, gas mark 6
- Place the tuna steaks onto a baking tray with a little olive oil. Put into the oven for approx 12 mins. Turn over halfway through. Cool, then roughly chop
- Lightly fry the onion with a little olive oil for 2 mins
- Stir in the pepper until slightly coloured – approx 5 mins. Cool
- To make the white sauce: warm the milk, set aside. Melt the margarine in a small saucepan. When melted add the flour and cook for 1 min
- Gradually add the milk – keep stirring whilst adding the milk. Stir in the salt, pepper and mustard. When all the milk has been used, the sauce should look thick and glossy. Cool slightly
- Transfer the onions and peppers, tuna, cooked pasta, herbs into a large bowl, then stir in the sauce evenly. Arrange neatly in a medium sized ovenproof dish
- Sprinkle the cheese over the top then transfer to the oven for approx 8 mins until the cheese has melted

560 Kcals per serving

> *When I was 15 years old I lived in a secure unit; I lived there for one year. This is when I started to learn to cook.*
>
> *To start with I did this because there was nothing to do and I was bored. The thing is that I began to really enjoy the sessions. I also felt happy because the sessions were one to one, so I was given lots of help.*
>
> *When I feel down I think of this happy time.*

Chicken curry

Serves 4

Ingredients

4 large chicken breasts – cut into large chunks, or 1 medium whole chicken – portioned
2 large green chillis – roughly sliced
2 medium sized fresh tomatoes – roughly chopped
1½ tablespoons basaar
4 medium sized onions – peeled and roughly chopped
1 thumb-sized piece ginger – peeled and sliced
1 bulb garlic – crushed and peeled
1 large handful fresh coriander – washed and roughly chopped
2 tablespoons olive oil
1 teaspoon garam masala
Pinch of salt to taste
300ml / ½ pint cold water

Method

- Place onion in large saucepan with olive oil, cook until soft, about 5 mins
- Add garlic and ginger, stir in tomatoes, basaar and salt
- Add half of the cold water
- Stir in chicken, simmer for 10 mins with lid on
- Add remaining water
- Simmer approx 15 mins, until sauce has thickened slightly
- Stir in the chillis and coriander
- Add garam masala

Serve with chapatti (see page 63)

248 Kcals per serving

Lasagne

Serves 6

Ingredients

For Bolognese sauce

500g / 1lb 2oz minced beef
1 large onion – peeled and roughly chopped
1 400g tin of chopped tomatoes
2 fresh tomatoes – roughly chopped
Pinch of dried mixed herbs
Large handful mushrooms, peeled and roughly
chopped
1 red pepper – deseeded and roughly chopped
3 cloves of garlic – crushed, peeled and roughly
chopped
Pinch of salt and pepper
1–2 glasses of water

Lasagne sheets – approx 8–9

For cheese sauce

1 tablespoon cornflour – mixed to a paste with
a little water
1 large knob sunflower margarine
1 pint semi-skimmed milk (you may need
more, I often make mine too thick!)
50g / 2oz cheddar – grated (I prefer red)
Pinch of salt and pepper

625 Kcals per serving

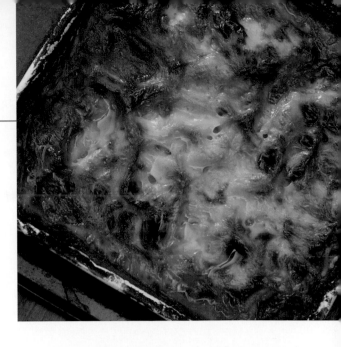

Method

- Preheat oven to 190ºC, 375ºF, gas mark 5

For Bolognese sauce
- Place onion and garlic in a large saucepan with olive oil, sauté until soft not brown – 5 mins
- Stir in the pepper, mushrooms then the minced beef until meat becomes brown in appearance
- Add the fresh and tinned tomatoes, then add mixed herbs, salt and pepper, then add the water
- Simmer on a low heat for about 30–45 mins until rich tomato red colour is achieved. Stir occasionally

For cheese sauce
- Heat milk gently in a pan
- Stir in the cornflour paste until it becomes slightly thickened, add the margarine, then stir in the cheese and season with the salt and pepper
- Continue stirring until smooth and glossy

(for an alternative way to make this cheese sauce see page 91)

To assemble
- Using a medium sized ovenproof dish, layer the Bolognese, lasagne and the cheese sauce – start with the Bolognese and use a layer of each twice, finishing with the cheese sauce
- Place in the oven for approx 30–45 mins until golden brown in appearance and lasagne sheets are soft and cooked through

> " This was the first thing I cooked for my ex-husband. He said that he didn't like lasagne – that was until he tasted mine!
>
> When I had my baby, lasagne was one of the things that I weaned her on – she loved it, and still loves it – she is nearly 10 years old. "

Chicken, lamb or mutton moghlai biryani

Serves 6

Ingredients

500g / 1lb 2oz chicken, lamb or mutton
450g / 1lb basmati rice
3 onions
1 inch piece of root ginger – peeled
3 cloves of garlic – crushed and peeled
4 red chillies
5 green chillies
225g / 9oz curds or natural yoghurt
Garlic – 6 flakes
5 cardamoms
5 cloves
2 cinnamon sticks
2 bay leaves
½ teaspoon cumin seeds
1 large handful of lightly toasted almonds, peanuts and cashews (lightly toasted by placing on a baking tray and put in oven at moderate temperature for 6–7 mins)
1 lime – juice
2 tablespoons desi ghee or clarified butter – set some aside for layering
2 tablespoons olive oil
Pinch of saffron dissolved in 12 teaspoons milk
A few drops of orange colouring
Pinch of garam masala
Bunch of fresh coriander – roughly chopped
Sprig of fresh mint leaves – roughly chopped
Pinch of salt to taste

Preparation

- Wash, clean and cut the chicken, lamb or mutton into chunks

- Peel and slice onions

- Grind ginger, garlic, green and red chillies, ideally in a pestle and mortar. Add curds or natural yoghurt and mix to a fine paste

- Marinate meat in above curds/natural yoghurt masala for 3–4 hours

Method

- Heat desi ghee or clarified butter and fry the sliced onions until crisp. Keep aside

- Put in the marinated meat in a large pan and cook until light brown. Chicken will take approximately 15–20 mins. Lamb or mutton will need longer – add a cup of water and stew for a further 25 mins. Keep aside

- Put the bay leaves, cardamoms, cloves, cinnamon sticks, garlic flakes and cumin seeds in a pan with the olive oil

- Add washed rice and lightly fry for about 5 mins, stirring continuously. Put in double the volume of rice of water (approximately 4 cups) and lime juice. Cook for about 8–10 mins till rice is just done

- When done, mix rice with chopped mint and coriander leaves

680 Kcals per serving

Layering

- Using a deep ovenproof dish such as a borosil or Pyrex dish put a layer of rice, saffron milk, desi ghee or clarified butter, fried onions, a little garam masala powder. Then a layer of cooked meat (chicken, lamb or mutton)

- Repeat procedure once more and then finish with a layer of rice and fried onions and remaining saffron milk

- Sprinkle on very tiny specks of orange food colouring, which spreads nicely when steamed

- Cover with a fitted lid then seal with kneaded atta dough – rolled out into a long rod shape, long enough to fit round the lid snugly. (Please see recipe for chapatti on page 63). By using the atta dough around the lid the moisture stays in the ovenproof dish and the biryani won't become dry

- Place in oven for about 20 mins

- Put the roasted nuts on top and serve hot

My tip: Fresh, chopped coriander will make a huge difference to an Indian recipe

Enjoy!! Good luck

"

I was born and raised in India, for the most part in the capital New Delhi, although I spent about five years in Poona (Western India) whilst at university. At the age of 25 I moved to the UK to complete my education and seek fame and fortune!

The India that I left some 30 years ago was a different place to what it is today. In New Delhi today, weather aside, you could be forgiven for thinking you were in any international capital. When I was growing up there, staple foods were an Indian bread, rice, dhal and one or two vegetable dishes. Meat, chicken etc were considered luxuries for special occasions, because an average family could not afford to buy meat regularly. Eating out too was a luxury. Five star hotels would have 'international' restaurants but these were out of the reach of the majority of Indian households.

When I arrived in the UK, one of the first noticeable differences between India and the UK was the food. Having hitherto been so used to my mother's quite spicy cooking, I was struck by the blandness of the food (although people would say to me that you were really experiencing food in its natural state and flavour, without the addition of condiments and spices!). I found food combinations such as curry sauce and chips curious – I might have had chips once or twice a year as a treat before I came to the UK. One really striking observation of that time was that if you were a vegetarian, you were certain to struggle to find something to eat if you went out.

With the demands of working and studying, I had to rely on hospital food and takeaway food as I had little time or inclination to cook for myself. Over a period of time I got used to the food, indeed started enjoying ham with parsley sauce and chips or beef stew with parsley dumplings!

After I first arrived in the UK in the early 1980s, I wasn't able to visit India for four or five years. In time I finished my further studies. During this period, my mother and sister visited me on a couple of occasions and would often cook meals whilst staying with me. They would find sourcing particular ingredients and spices difficult, and choice was limited further because my mother was vegetarian (although she would cook non-vegetarian food for us), making going out for a meal quite challenging. My mother's cooking re-awoke many happy times – remembering biryani dishes at special occasions and staples such as dhal and chapattis – this was the catalyst that made me want to learn how to cook.

To start with I would either follow my mother's methods of cooking or would use a recipe and follow it rigidly. As I became more confident I would adapt recipes and follow my intuition.

I have been married for quite a number of years, and I would say that I do quite a lot of the cooking for my family. I still enjoy cooking Indian food but my tastes are quite varied now – enjoying British roasts, earthy European stews (always with dumplings – mmmmm) and Italian and Mexican dishes. I have failed singularly to produce an authentic Chinese meal and I cannot get myself to try a battered Mars bar!

"

Jollof rice: the soul food!

Serves 4–6

Ingredients

¼ cup olive oil
750g / 1½ lb chicken, cut into pieces
5 cups water or stock
2 onions, chopped
1 red or green bell pepper, roughly chopped
3–4 cloves garlic, crushed, peeled and minced or finely chopped
3 cups long grain rice
¼ cups tomato paste/puree
2 cups fresh tomatoes, roughly chopped
2 carrots, peeled and chopped
1 cup green beans
1 cup cabbage, chopped/shredded
Salt and pepper to taste

Method

* Parboil your rice in a pan with water for 10 mins with medium heat

* In a separate pan or wok, heat 2–3 teaspoons of oil over a medium heat. Add the onions, diced chicken and peppers and sauté until the onions are tender and translucent, about 4–5 mins

* Add the garlic and fry for another 1–2 mins

* Stir the rice into the onions and peppers and heat through for another 1–2 mins

* Stir in the tomato paste/puree to coat the rice and give it a reddish hue. Add the chopped tomatoes and let them cook down for 2–3 mins

* Pour the warmed stock or water into the rice pot and add the carrots, green beans and cabbage. Season well with salt and pepper

* Bring to the boil, reduce heat to low, cover tightly and simmer for 20 mins or until water has almost evaporated

* Remove from heat, let rice rest another 10 mins

* Remove to a serving platter and serve with dodo (fried plantains), sliced hard-boiled eggs and a side salad

603 Kcals per average serving

"

Jollof rice is a dish eaten commonly in the sub–Saharan Africa. Jollof rice originated from the West African region but is more cooked in Nigeria. It is easily prepared but deeply symbolic. Its symbolism is not in the uniqueness of the cooking or the ingredients. It is what it represents for the people of that region – the sense of community togetherness, welcome, openness, transparency, support and collective well-being for the community.

I come from Eastern Nigeria where the spoken language is Ibo and the population is largely Catholic.

Family units are large and the sense of communities and value ties are entrenched. Hence, families spend Monday to Saturday working at their various trades. All rested on Sunday. Therefore, Sundays are marked by going to church in the morning. Lunchtime is usually marked by a meal of hot spicy jollof rice garnished with fried plantain and coleslaw and salad. This is akin to the English Sunday roast.

At Sunday lunches you have several generations of a family on the table. A lot of family advice, support, confiding, 'telling off' of younger kids by adults, updating, enquiries about general well-being, pastoral duties by the older adults to the younger ones goes on as the bowls of the ubiquitous Jollof rice is wolfed down.

Even if for some bizarre reasons your folks are not around on a Sunday to cook Sunday lunch, you can be guaranteed a bowl of jollof rice should you pop round to Mama Ngozi's or Papa Ada's house. One does not need an invitation to lunch; hence on Sundays, at about lunchtime, you have endless streams of aunts/uncles/cousins coming in for a bowl of jollof rice and some pieces of advice from the elderly. The meal is prepared in a huge wok-like pan and the quantity is always large enough to feed at least 30 people.

In time, I grew up and left home to go to university. After university, I decided to see the world, and hence travelled abroad to various countries: Gambia, Ghana, South Africa, the US, Canada, London. I was pleasantly surprised to find that jollof rice remains ubiquitous within the Nigerians in these areas. They cook it mostly on Sundays as we did back home, with yet again many pastoral discussions and duties being held as the bowls of jollof rice are eaten. It has to be said that no Nigerian occasions take place without the host preparing a dish of jollof rice.

As I now live far away from home, I have come to associate jollof rice with community togetherness, feelings of being supported and looked after, and a sense of mental well-being as I always feel refreshed and ready to face the battle anytime I go to Nigerians' houses to eat jollof rice. This is not to do with the ingredients in jollof rice but the milieu in which it is eaten. It kind of liberates people and they speak to each other, ask what your worries are and generally look after each other's mental well-being as we eat jollof rice. Such occasions remind me of what one of my non-Nigerian friends once remarked: that it is like the soul food – it recharges one's battery – not the food itself but the general well-being chats that go on as it is consumed.

"

> 66
>
> *This recipe reminds me of when I was a child: a memory of when I used to go to my grandma's and help her with her housework and her gardening.*
>
> *She would ask me what I would like to eat. She would give me the choice of stew and Yorkshire pudding or the choice of chips and sausage. I would always choose stew and Yorkshire pudding as it's my favourite and my grandma knows that.*
>
> *When I get released from this hospital I will be straight to my grandma's for her stew and Yorkshire pudding and for the good memories.*
>
> 99

Grandma's stew with Yorkshire pudding

Serves 4

Ingredients

250g / 10 oz minced lamb or beef
450g / 1lb new or old potatoes – roughly chopped
Large handful of frozen peas
3 medium sized carrots – peeled and cut into rounds
2 sticks of celery – roughly chopped
1 medium sized onion – peeled and roughly chopped
1 tablespoon cornflour – made to a paste with a little cold water
2 beef or lamb stock cubes – diluted in 1 pint boiling water
A few sprigs of fresh mint
1 tablespoon olive oil
Pinch of salt and pepper

Method

- Preheat oven to 190⁰C, 375⁰F, gas mark 5
- Wash the vegetables
- In a large pan put in the olive oil, then add the onion, carrots, celery and pinch of salt. Sweat off for approx 8 mins
- Add mince, cook until brown
- Stir in the potatoes
- Add stock (may need a little more water at some point) mint and pepper
- Simmer for approx 45 mins
- Thicken stew with cornflour (may not need all the cornflour)

Yorkshire pudding

Makes 1 large pudding

Ingredients

1½ cups plain flour
300ml / ½ pint cold milk
Pinch of salt and pepper
3 medium sized eggs
2 tablespoons olive oil

Method

- Whisk eggs in a small bowl or measuring jug
- Gradually add the flour, beat until smooth
- Gradually add the milk until mixture looks like a smooth batter
- Add salt and pepper
- Rest in the fridge for about 30 mins
- Place olive oil in a small baking tin
- Place in oven for about 5–8 mins until hot
- Carefully take out of oven and pour the batter into the tin
- Place in oven for approx 20–25 mins, until well risen, golden in colour and crisp in texture

My tip:
Serve with Grandma's stew in the middle – Enjoy!

513 Kcals per serving

A fisherman's breakfast

Serves 2

Ingredients

2 portions of cod roe – fresh preferably, but you can use tinned,
sliced into 2 portions
2 eggs
2 rashers smoked bacon – chopped
Dash of olive oil
2 large handfuls of spinach – washed and wilted (see back of
packet for instructions)
2 radishes – grated

Method

- Fry the cod roe for 1 minute on each side until lightly golden
  in colour
- Next poach the egg. Carefully crack the egg into boiling
  water and poach for about 4–5 mins
- Fry the chopped bacon in a little olive oil for 2–3 mins, until
  crispy. Drain well on kitchen paper
- Place the cod roe in the middle of the plate
- Put spinach on top, then carefully place the poached egg on
  top of the spinach
- Next, sprinkle the bacon and radish over the top of the
  prepared meal

230 Kcals per serving

"

Memories of a bygone age.

My dad was a fisherman. This meant that he would often be away from home for three weeks at a time.

This recipe is a typical fisherman's breakfast which all my family used to eat, especially when my dad returned home.

I don't have any photos of my mum and dad – when I eat this meal, nice memories of my family come flooding back. "

> *This dish is a favourite of my grandparent's generation and reminds me of times spent by the coast where it is possible to get hold of really fresh seafood.*
>
> *This dish is great from a nutritional perspective, which is important to me. It is a balanced meal within itself because it contains protein (seafood, dairy, and egg), carbohydrate (potato) and vegetables (peas and leeks).*
>
> *It contains a good amount of protein, which is really important for recovery and growth.*
>
> *Using salmon rather than smoked haddock means the dish will also contain Omega 3 fatty acids which are good for the heart and joints.*

Seaside fish pie

Feeds up to 6 people

Ingredients

350g / 12oz skinless white fish e.g. haddock, coley or cod
350g / 12oz salmon or skinless smoked haddock
570ml / 1 pint milk
100g / 4oz butter
50g / 2oz plain flour
1 medium leek, finely sliced and washed
175g / 6oz cooked, peeled prawns
200g / 8oz frozen or fresh peas
3 hard-boiled eggs – peeled and quartered
Juice of half a lemon
Salt and pepper

For the topping

1.5kg / 3lb boiled potatoes
50ml / 3 tablespoons milk
50g / 2oz grated cheese

Method

- Preheat oven to 200⁰C, 400⁰F, gas mark 6
- Place the fish in a baking dish and pour over half the milk
- Dot the fish with 25g (1oz) butter and season with salt and pepper. Bake in the oven for 15–20 mins
- Drain the milk from the fish, saving it for later. Remove any skin from the fish and break fish into large pieces
- To make the sauce, melt the remaining 75g (3oz) butter in a pan. Remove the pan from the heat and stir in the flour. Return the pan to the heat and gradually add the milk (beginning with the milk used to cook the fish)
- Season with salt and pepper
- Spread the leeks over the base of the baking dish. Add the fish, prawns, peas and egg. Sprinkle with the lemon juice before pouring the sauce over the fish
- Mash the potatoes with 50ml (3 tablespoons) of milk, season with salt and pepper
- Spread the potato over the fish mixture and sprinkle with cheese
- Bake the fish pie in the oven for 30–40 minutes until hot throughout and browned on top

My tip: Fish pie is usually served with peas but would also work well with wilted spinach, broccoli or a simple salad

Bon appétit!

650 Kcals per serving

109

Jerk chicken with rice and peas

Serves 2

Ingredients

2–3 chicken breasts – washed and cut into pieces
1 lime – juice
Pinch of salt
1 small 200g tin black-eyed peas or cow peas
300ml / ½ pint water
½ green chilli – chopped
3 shallots – peeled and finely chopped
2 cups long grain rice – white or brown
1 small handful fresh thyme
1 small 200g tin coconut milk
Pinch of sugar

For the jerk marinade
A thumb-sized piece of root ginger – peeled and sliced
1 lime – juice
2 cloves garlic – crushed and peeled
2 spring onions – sliced
1 teaspoon olive oil
1 dessertspoon water
½ green chilli – sliced
1 teaspoon allspice
1 dessertspoon soya sauce
Pinch of salt

Blend all the marinade ingredients together until smooth

Method
- Preheat oven to 190°C, 375°F, gas mark 5
- Put chicken in a bowl
- Squeeze lime juice over the chicken
- Add pinch of salt
- Mix in the jerk marinade
- Leave to marinate for as long as you can (ideally overnight)
- Transfer chicken to a baking tray and cook for between 30–45 mins

For the rice and peas
- Place the shallot, chilli, thyme, coconut milk, water and peas in a large pan. Simmer for approx 45 mins until peas are soft
- Stir in rice and salt (may need a little more water). Cook until rice softens and water almost evaporates

My tip: Serve with green salad and rice and peas, or a potato salad

535 Kcals per serving

"I love football as much as my mother's jerk chicken."

> My mother used to cook for the local church. Her food was so good that I remember her entering a competition at the church fête and winning a holiday.
>
> My family would often hire the church hall for family celebrations such as special birthdays, and there used be so much lovely food to eat, like bun and cheese, mutton, fish, beef and dumplings. This is when I learnt to cook – I was about 15 and would help my mother with the preparations.
>
> The meal that comes to mind when I think of happy times is jerk chicken, served with green salad and rice and peas. My family would eat this together at 4 o'clock when I came home from school.

“

This recipe is one of my mum's favourite recipes; it is also one of mine, because salmon is my favourite fish.

I am very close to my mum. In my family it is my mum who is the traditionalist and sets the tone when we have a get-together.

At Christmas time me and my son stay at my mum's house. We have a lovely time. The family festivities have always started on Christmas Eve, where we sit down in the evening and enjoy Christmas dinner. This usually comprises of pheasant with all the trimmings!

Christmas Day always involves a cooked breakfast followed by a buffet later in the day. My mum does this rather than a Christmas dinner, so that the family can have time to open presents and enjoy each other's company.

On Boxing Day we usually cook this salmon recipe. When I eat this it always reminds me of my family and Christmas time, and I think about my mum and her traditions and individuality – even down to her always setting the table with a lace tablecloth over a pink one!

”

Mum's salmon celebration

Serves 2

Ingredients

2 salmon fillets
300ml / 10fl oz semi-skimmed milk

1 large handful of new potatoes – washed
then boiled in a pan for 10–15 mins, until soft
1 large handful asparagus or green beans –
lightly steamed for 4–5 mins

For the sauce

25g / 1oz butter
1 tablespoon plain flour
1 matchbox size piece of Cheddar cheese –
grated
1 small packet of king prawns
Pinch of salt and pepper

Method

- Poach the salmon in the milk in a medium
  sized saucepan for approximately 8–10
  minutes. Set aside

To make the sauce

- Melt the butter in a saucepan then stir in
  the flour
- Gradually add the milk that has been
  used to poach the salmon until the sauce
  is smooth and glossy in appearance – no
  lumps!
- Add the cheese, prawns, salt and pepper
- Arrange on a plate with the new potatoes
  and asparagus, and serve

568 Kcals per serving

My parents' shop, taken in the 1960s

> My parents were in business – they owned and ran a successful greengrocer and all-purpose store in the 1960s.
>
> As my mother and father were so busy, we didn't have home-cooked food at home. Instead, I remember eating Birds Eye™ oven-prepared meals (nowadays these would usually be cooked using a microwave). My mother would place the meal on the table. It was contained in a tin foil tray – I would then wash the tray and take it to school, where it was used in painting activities.
>
> I would often go to my grandma's house for tea. My grandma would make things like oxtail and shin beef, finny haddock, jam roly-poly and bubble and squeak. All the produce used was from my parents' shop.
>
> All the family would get together at Grandma's house at Christmas and Easter time. At celebratory times Grandma would set the oak table and pull up the drop-leaves to make the table bigger.

Grandma's bubble and squeak

An ideal recipe to use with leftover cooked vegetables

Ingredients

Leftover cooked vegetables from the day before – e.g. potatoes, swede, cabbage, carrots, Brussels sprouts
Pinch of salt and pepper
A little olive oil

Method

- Place all the ingredients in a bowl and carefully mash and mix together. Add a pinch of salt and pepper
- Put olive oil in a large frying pan and heat slightly
- Add the mixture and fry on a medium heat, stirring gently for approximately 5–8 mins until the bubble and squeak is golden brown in colour

Serve on its own or with cooked meat or fish

My tip: To make the bubble and squeak look extra special, shape into small pattie shapes before frying.

215 Kcals per pattie

Salt fish and ackee

Serves 4–6

Ingredients

450g / 1lb salt cod – soaked in cold water overnight
1 large onion – peeled and roughly chopped
1–2 scotch bonnet chillies – finely chopped
1 clove of garlic – crushed, peeled and chopped
1 large red pepper – deseeded and roughly chopped
1 large green pepper – deseeded and roughly chopped
4 large fresh tomatoes – roughly chopped
1 small handful fresh thyme – chopped finely
1 tablespoon olive oil
1 280g tin ackee – drained
Pinch of salt and pepper

Method

- Drain the water from the fish and simmer in a pan with fresh cold water for about 20 mins
- Meanwhile, sauté the scotch bonnet chillies, green and red peppers, onion and garlic in the olive oil for about 8 mins
- Stir in the thyme, tomatoes, salt and pepper and sauté for a further 8 mins
- Drain the fish, cool slightly, then flake into the rest of the ingredients and stir
- Gently stir in the ackee, being careful not to break it up too much

My tip: Serve with dumplings, rice and peas (See page 191)

328 Kcals per average serving

"I would recommend this dish to anybody who loves Caribbean food

> This recipe reminds me of when I would come home from school and Mother would be cooking this meal for the family. We would then all sit down together to eat and enjoy Mum's cooking.
>
> My mother was Jamaican born and bred and these were the type of dishes that she would cook for the family.
>
> I have never really cooked much before but what I have learnt has come from years of watching my mother and aunties in the kitchen.
>
> My goal is to visit Jamaica one day and to experience the food and discover the roots of my mother's cooking.
>
> My mother was fantastic in cooking and as a person. "

66

As a child I always remember eating mince and tatties with my family. My mother would cook the meal and all the family would sit together at teatime.

I had a healthy appetite and would often eat my brothers' or sisters' leftovers, but never became fat. We didn't eat lots of snacks – we would fill up on extra vegetables.

I have happy memories of my mother's cooking – I can still smell and taste it to this day!

If I feel low or sad I remember these happy times.

99

Mince and tatties

Serves 4

Ingredients

For the mince

1 onion – red or white – roughly chopped
2 medium sized carrots – roughly diced
1 beef stock cube made up with 1 litre / 2 pints water
500g / 1lb 2oz lean minced beef
1 tablespoon olive oil
1 dessertspoon cornflour and gravy powder – mixed to a paste
with 2 tablespoons cold water

For the mashed tatties

6 medium sized potatoes – peeled and roughly chopped
Knob of butter/sunflower margarine
Splash of semi-skimmed milk

Method

For the mince

- Gently fry the onions in the olive oil until soft – 3 mins
- Add the carrots, stir for 3–5 mins
- Add the meat and cook until brown – 8 mins
- Cover with stock and simmer for approx 1½ hours
- Thicken with the gravy powder and cornflour
- Season with a pinch of salt and pepper

For the mashed tatties

- Place the potatoes in a medium sized pan, cover with water and boil on a high heat until soft – approx 20 mins
- Drain the potatoes. Using a potato masher, mash until smooth
- Add butter/margarine and milk, and a pinch of salt and pepper

My tip: *Serve with peas*

558 Kcals per serving

Chicken masala

Serves 4–5

Ingredients

4–6 chicken breasts – roughly diced
4 large onions – roughly chopped
1 bulb garlic – crushed and peeled
1½ tablespoons basaar
1 teaspoon garam masala
2 large fresh tomatoes – sliced
4 fresh green chillies
1 large handful coriander – chopped
Cold water – 2 glasses
2–3 tablespoons olive oil
Pinch of salt

Method

- Put oil into a medium sized pan then add onion and garlic, fry gently for approx 5–8 mins until soft
- Add basaar and salt
- Stir in the tomatoes, cook for 8 mins
- Add water, simmer for 5 mins
- Add the chicken and stir occasionally until sauce is reduced in volume – about 20 mins
- Stir in the coriander and green chillies
- Just before serving add garam masala

Serve with chapatti (see page 63)

305 Kcals per average serving

My family moved to England from Pakistan when I was five.

At this time in my life I remember going to school and feeling different. Some of the other children bullied me. This used to really upset me – I just couldn't understand why they would do such a thing.

My parents told me to tell the teachers – but the bullying didn't stop. In the end I dealt with the problem by skipping school. I learnt to get by, and learnt basic English from my big brother.

This meal is one of my favourites. When I was older I cooked this for my family in the restaurant I worked in, and sometimes my wife would cook it. It brings back good memories.

Beef stew and dumplings

Serves 4–6

Ingredients

For the stew

500g / 1lb 2oz beef (stewing, skirt, braising or casserole) – cut into bite-sized chunks
450g /1lb potatoes – cut into chunks
1 leek – cut into slices
3 parsnips – cut into chunks
4 large carrots – peeled and cut into slices
1 large onion – peeled and roughly chopped
Pinch of salt and pepper
2 tablespoons olive oil
1 tablespoon cornflour – mixed to a paste with cold water
1 beef stock cube – mixed into 1 litre / 2 pints of boiling water

For the dumplings

50g / 2oz vegetable suet
100g / 4oz self-raising flour
Pinch of salt and pepper
Cold water – enough to make into a dough

Method

- Fry the onion and leek in a large saucepan on a medium heat with 1 tablespoon olive oil. Stir until soft, about 5–8 mins
- Add the carrots and parsnips and stir for a further 5 mins, then add the potatoes and stir for another 5 mins
- Meanwhile, in a frying pan seal the beef on a medium heat with the remaining olive oil – this should take about 8–10 mins
- Transfer the meat to the saucepan and mix evenly into the vegetables
- Stir in the stock and simmer for between 2 to 3 hours on a low heat with the lid on, stirring occasionally (you might need to add more water during this process)
- The beef should now be tender. Add the cornflour to thicken the stew

To make the dumplings

- Place all the dry ingredients into a mixing bowl. Mix in enough water to form a soft dough. Knead slightly
- Transfer the dough onto a floured surface. Cut into 6–8 portions. Roll into balls, carefully place into the stew and place lid back onto the pan. Cook for about 25 mins until the dumplings have nearly doubled in size

My tip: *Serve with cabbage and crusty bread to mop up the gravy!*

512 Kcals per average serving

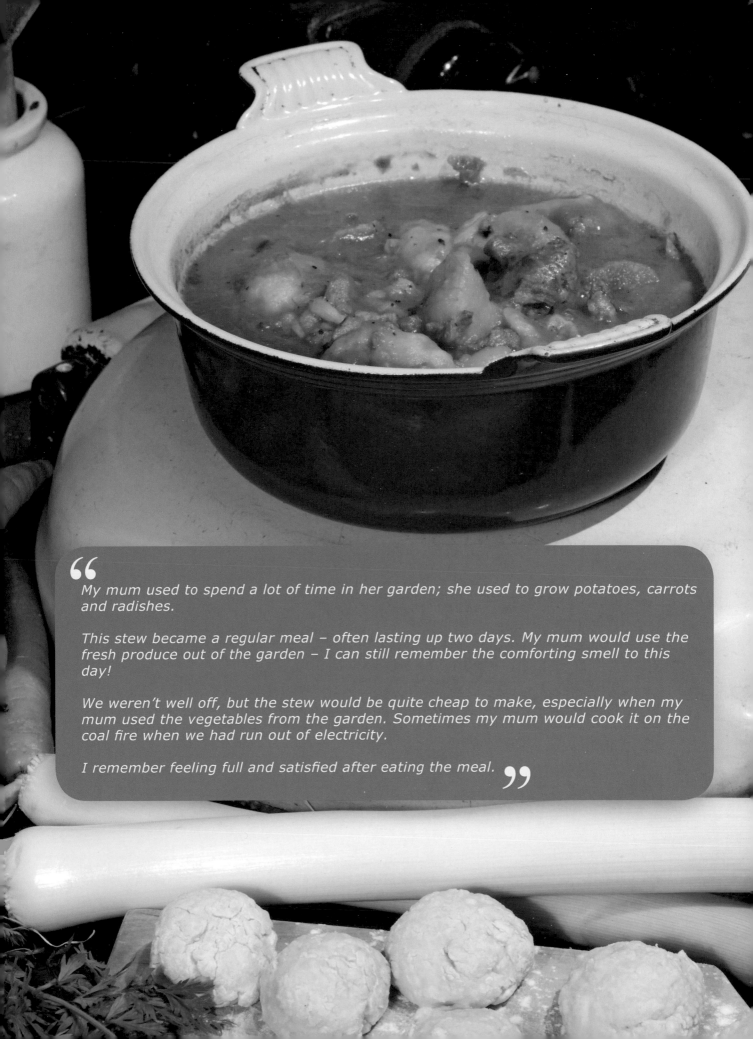

> My mum used to spend a lot of time in her garden; she used to grow potatoes, carrots and radishes.
>
> This stew became a regular meal – often lasting up two days. My mum would use the fresh produce out of the garden – I can still remember the comforting smell to this day!
>
> We weren't well off, but the stew would be quite cheap to make, especially when my mum used the vegetables from the garden. Sometimes my mum would cook it on the coal fire when we had run out of electricity.
>
> I remember feeling full and satisfied after eating the meal.

Chicken korma

Serves 2

Ingredients

2 skinless and boneless chicken breasts, diced
1 medium sized onion – peeled and finely chopped
1 clove of garlic – crushed, peeled and finely chopped
1 chicken stock cube diluted in 150ml / ¼ pint hot water from the kettle
1 tablespoon creamed coconut
1 large handful fresh coriander
2–4 tablespoons mild curry powder
1 tablespoon olive oil
½ red chilli (optional) – finely chopped
2 tablespoons natural yoghurt

Method

- Put oil in a saucepan until it is sizzling and then add the chicken. Cook until browned, on a medium heat
- Add the onion and the garlic and cook until soft
- Prepare stock separately and then add to the saucepan
- Add all other ingredients apart from the yogurt
- Turn down the heat and cover, leave to simmer for around 30–40 minutes
- Turn the heat off and add the yoghurt, then stir it well

Serve with naan bread (see page 69)

340 Kcals per serving

Chicken korma brings back happy times when I used to work in a mental health unit before I became unwell.

I remember the camaraderie between the staff to work hard to get the workload done. We would also take it in turns to make a meal that we could all eat and enjoy – such a treat – especially when working a night shift!

Picture taken from a family holiday

> I grew up with my mum and dad, two brothers and two sisters.
>
> This recipe was a favourite of mine. Originally my mum made it, but when my dad learnt to make it, it tasted so much better!
>
> My dad died of cancer. When I think of eating my dad's shepherd's pie I have fond memories of my dad, school and family holidays on the Yorkshire coast.

126

Dad's shepherd's pie

Serves 4–6

Ingredients

500g / 1lb 2oz minced lamb
1 large onion – peeled and finely chopped
4 medium sized carrots – cut into rounds
2 large handfuls frozen garden peas
1 lamb or beef stock cube sprinkled into 1 litre / 2 pints boiling water
1 dessertspoon cornflour
1 dessertspoon of gravy granules/powder – mixed with the cornflour to a paste
with a little cold water
1 tablespoon olive oil
Pinch of salt and pepper

For the top

900g / 2lbs potatoes – peeled and cut into chunks
Splash of semi-skimmed milk
Knob of butter or sunflower margarine

1 matchbox size of mature Cheddar cheese – grated

Method

- Preheat oven to 180ºC, 350ºF, gas mark 4

- Fry the onion in a saucepan with the olive oil on a medium heat until soft – about 5–8 mins. Add the carrots, stir for a couple of minutes

- Add the minced lamb, cook until brown – about 8–10 mins

- Add the peas, then add the stock. Simmer for approximately 30–40 mins – add more water if necessary. Add salt and pepper

- Meanwhile, put the potatoes in a large saucepan, cover with cold water and a pinch of salt and boil gently for approximately 20–25 mins until soft

- Drain the potatoes (you might want to use some of the water to add to the mince). Using a potato masher, mash the potatoes until free from lumps. Add the butter and milk

- Going back to the mince, thicken the meat with the cornflour and gravy granules/powder

- Using a slotted spoon (spoon with holes in it!) transfer the meat with a little gravy into an ovenproof dish or tin

- Carefully place the mashed potato over the top and decorate using a fork

- Sprinkle the cheese evenly over the top

- Place in the oven for about 30–35 mins until golden brown in colour

- Remove and leave to settle for about 10 mins

My tip: Serve with broccoli

529 Kcals per average serving

When I was growing up I remember vividly the lovely smell of dinner cooking on a Sunday morning. Me and my brother would wait patiently for the dinner to be ready, even though it seemed to take ages, and I remember feeling so hungry whilst waiting.

My aim is to taste my mum's Sunday dinner again. I have asked her if she would do it again for me when I move on, and she has said yes.

My mum's Sunday dinner

This is my artwork

Serves 4

Ingredients

1 whole chicken
Homemade sage and onion stuffing recipe – see page 190
Yorkshire pudding recipe – see page 192
4 small handfuls of Brussels sprouts – fresh or frozen. Discard any
brown outer leaves then make an incision at the bottom of each
sprout
4 large carrots – peeled and cut into rounds
4–5 large potatoes – peeled and cut into chunks

Gravy – 2 tablespoons gravy powder or granules and 1 tablespoon cornflour – mixed
to a paste with cold water

Method

- Preheat the oven to 190⁰C, 375⁰F, gas mark 5

- Transfer the chicken – as per instructions on the packet – onto a roasting tin.
  Roast the chicken in the oven: 20 mins per 450g / 1lb, plus an extra 20 mins.
  For example a large chicken weighing 2.2kg / 5lb will take about 2 hours. Cool
  slightly, then carve into slices

- While the chicken is roasting, prepare the rest of the meal. Parboil the potatoes
  for about 10 mins then drain (save the potato water for the gravy). Transfer the
  drained potatoes around the chicken for about ¾–1 hour until golden in colour,
  turn occasionally

- Put the carrots in a medium sized saucepan and boil in water for about 10–15
  mins until just turning soft – check by inserting a fork. Drain (save the water for
  the gravy)

- Place the Brussels sprouts in a saucepan of boiling water and boil for about 5–10
  mins until just turning soft – check by inserting a fork. Drain (save the water for
  the gravy)

- To make the gravy, place all the saved vegetable stock into a saucepan. If
  desired, add some of the cooked chicken meat juices. Thicken the stock with the
  gravy granules and cornflour – keep stirring until thickened, then simmer for 5
  mins

- Arrange the prepared meal on plates and serve

511 Kcals per serving

"This recipe is tasty and delicious and I think I was
the one who invented it!"

Since I've been married, this is the one dish that my wife is happy
for me to cook – I am often forgetful and have been close to
creating a fire in the kitchen as a result.

I have been making this dish for a number of years – it is quick,
easy and wholesome. I find that it gives me pleasure when making
it. My mother came to stay recently and I cooked it for her. She
enjoyed it – it is a moreish dish.

Corned beef pie

Serves 3–4

Ingredients

1 200g tin of good quality corned beef – chopped into small chunks
5 large potatoes – peeled and chopped
50g / 2oz Cheddar cheese – grated
2 large tomatoes– sliced
Knob of butter
Splash of semi-skimmed milk

Method

- Place the potatoes in a medium sized pan, fill the pan with cold water and boil for about 20–25 mins until soft. Carefully drain the water and mash with a potato masher. Add the butter and milk

- Meanwhile, put the corned beef into an ovenproof dish and place under the grill on a medium heat for 5–8 mins until the meat has softened

- Next mix the corned beef and mashed potato together and place back into the ovenproof dish

- Sprinkle half the cheese over the mixture

- Then arrange the tomato over the top, followed by the remaining cheese

- Put under the grill until golden in appearance – approx 5 mins

My tip: This is nice served with coleslaw

513 Kcals per average serving

Mutton curry

Serves 4–6

Ingredients

1 kg / 2lb 3oz mutton – prepared on the bone or deboned and diced
1 large onion – peeled and roughly chopped
4 fresh tomatoes – finely chopped
Pinch of salt and pepper
2 tablespoons of mild or hot curry powder
Large handful fresh thyme – roughly chopped
2 cups of hot water from the kettle
A little olive oil

Rice

2 cups of basmati rice – white or brown
1 tablespoon coconut milk/cream – tinned or packet
Cold water to cover the rice
Pinch of salt
3 tablespoons tinned kidney beans

Method

- Season mutton with salt and pepper. Add 1 dessertspoon of olive oil. Marinate for half an hour
- Transfer the mutton into a large saucepan with a drizzle of olive oil, stir until meat has browned, approx 10–15 mins
- Next add the onions, tomatoes and thyme. Stir for approx 6 mins then add curry powder
- Stir in the water and simmer on a low heat for approx 1½–2 hours, until meat is tender

For the rice

- Wash rice thoroughly
- Transfer to a medium sized saucepan, add the coconut milk/cream, water, salt and kidney beans
- Boil gently for approx 10 mins, until the liquid has evaporated and the rice is light and fluffy

132

501 Kcals per average serving

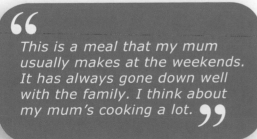

Authentic lamb kebabs

Makes 8

Ingredients

500g / 1lb 2oz minced lamb
1 onion – peeled and chopped finely
2 red chillies – chopped finely
4 cloves garlic – crushed, peeled and finely chopped
1 thumb-sized piece root ginger – peeled and finely chopped
½ teaspoon turmeric
1 medium sized egg – beaten
100g / 4oz gram flour
Pinch of salt and pepper
2 teaspoons garam masala
1 teaspoon cumin seeds
1 large handful fresh coriander – roughly chopped
1 tablespoon olive oil

Method

- Preheat the oven to 190⁰C, 375⁰F, gas mark 5
- Mix all the ingredients together in a large bowl
- Using your hands, and a little flour to stop the ingredients sticking, mould into sausage or burger shapes
- Place the olive oil into a large frying pan then carefully drop the prepared kebab ingredients into the oil to lightly brown – approx 5 mins
- Transfer onto a baking tray and place in the oven for approx 15 mins, until meat is cooked through and excess oil has drained into the baking tray

My tip: Serve in pitta bread with salad and raita

205 Kcals per kebab

> I remember eating lamb kebabs when I was younger – 9 years old. Both my mum and dad are very good cooks but this recipe was one that my mum learnt to cook and adapt from a family friend who was originally from India.

> When I eat this meal I remember my Uncle Pete. He used to come to our house and we would eat together.
>
> When we had a Chinese theme night at home, Uncle Pete would bring some curry sauce and my mum would supply everything else – including the chopsticks!
>
> My uncle died a few years ago and when I sit down and eat chicken chow mein fond memories of my Uncle Pete come back into my mind.

Chicken chow mein

Serves 2–3

Ingredients

150g / 6oz dried yellow shi wheat flour noodles (or fresh rice or egg noodles)
Dash of toasted sesame oil
300g / 12oz skinless chicken breast, sliced into strips
Dash of dark soy sauce
1 teaspoon five-spice powder
1 teaspoon chilli sauce (optional)
1 tablespoon groundnut oil
1 red pepper, deseeded and finely sliced
1 tablespoon cornflour
150g / 6oz bean sprouts
1 large spring onion, sliced lengthways
2 tablespoons light soy sauce
Freshly ground pepper

Method

- If using the dried noodles, cook in a pan of boiling water for 2–3 mins until al dente, or according to packet instructions. Drain, then rinse under cold running water and drain again. Drizzle with a dash of sesame oil and toss through to prevent noodles sticking to each other

- Put the chicken strips in a bowl and season with a dash of dark soy sauce, five-spice powder and chilli sauce, if using. Mix well then lightly dust the chicken with the cornflour

- Heat a wok or large frying pan and add the groundnut oil, then add the chicken and stir fry for approx 8 mins or until the chicken is golden brown and cooked through – depends how thinly the chicken is sliced

- Add the red pepper and stir fry for 3 mins, then add the bean sprouts and spring onion and stir fry for 2 mins

- Stir in the cooked shi wheat, rice or egg noodles and season with light soy sauce, a dash of sesame oil and ground black pepper

- Place the stir fry onto a serving plate and serve immediately

My tips:

— Instead of using chicken, try pork, fish or quorn

— You can use a wider selection of vegetables. I sometimes use ready prepared stir fry veg — fresh or frozen — which you can get from most supermarkets

— We like to eat this with curry sauce

— No need to add salt as soy sauce already contains salt

259 Kcals per average serving

Fishcakes

Makes 4

Ingredients

2 slices of bread – white or wholemeal
300g / 12oz fish fillets of your choice (skinned and boneless)
1 lemon – juice and zest
1 clove garlic (crushed)
Small handful parsley
Pinch of salt and pepper
1 egg – beaten
Flour to coat
Sunflower oil – 3 tablespoons

Method

- Blend bread until fine breadcrumbs
- Place the fish into a blender, grate the zest of the lemon and pull the leaves of parsley apart and add them to the other ingredients. Place the lid on the blender and pulse until coarsely mixed. Season with salt and pepper
- Add half of the breadcrumbs and pulse again a few more times, add lemon juice
- Remove all the mixture from the blender into a mixing bowl. Divide into 4 then shape into rounds using your hands, lightly covered in flour
- Beat the egg into a small mixing bowl
- Put the rest of the breadcrumbs into another bowl
- Take each fishcake and cover in flour, dip into the egg then coat in breadcrumbs
- Heat the oil in a frying pan on a medium heat. Place the garlic clove into the oil, lightly fry then remove
- Gently lower the fishcakes into the oil using a spatula. Cook for 8 mins, flip over and cook for another 8 mins
- Drain well on kitchen paper

My tip: If you don't have a blender, finely chop the ingredients then mix together

245 Kcals per fish cake

As an alternative try using oily fish
such as salmon or fresh tuna for the
omega 3 fatty acid health benefits
— see page 32

66
*Whilst I was growing up most of the
adult males in my family worked on
the trawlers. When they all came
home my nan was in the kitchen and
we all had fishcake and chips that
she made herself from the fish that
the guys had just brought in.*
99

Chicken tajen
with lemon preserve and green olives

Serves 4

Ingredients

1 medium sized chicken

To clean the chicken
150ml / ¼ pint vinegar
Cold water to rinse

For the chicken rub
Mix together:
Pinch of salt
1 teaspoon ground ginger
½ teaspoon turmeric
½ teaspoon Ras-el-hanout
1 tablespoon olive oil

2 lemons – sliced

For the preserved lemon and olive sauce
2 large red onions – peeled and finely
chopped (use a food processor if possible)
10 garlic cloves – crushed, peeled and finely
chopped (preferably in the food processor)
4 preserved lemons – skin only, cut into fine
strips (shop bought or homemade)
1 small tub/jar green olives (drained, rinsed
and boiled in water for approx 10 mins)
1½ teaspoons turmeric
Pinch of saffron (diluted in a tablespoon boiled
water)
Pinch of ginger and ground black pepper
2 tablespoons olive oil
1 large handful fresh coriander – roughly
chopped
2 cups water

My tips:

— This beautiful dish is nice eaten hot
or cold

— You can make your own preserved
lemons — they are so nice and don't
cost as much to make as the ones in
the shops

479 Kcals per serving

Method

- Wash the chicken with the vinegar, leave this for 10 mins and then wash off with cold water. Now cover the chicken in the meat rub and place the lemon slices over the chicken

- Place the chicken into a large food bag and seal well

- Place in the fridge to marinate – preferably overnight

- Take chicken out of fridge about 30 mins before cooking

- Preheat the oven to 220°C, 425°F, gas mark 7

- Place a drizzle of olive oil into a large saucepan over a medium heat. Carefully place the chicken into the hot oil. Keep moving the position of the chicken until it turns a light brown colour and caramalises evenly. Remove from heat

- Add a pinch of the listed spices (turmeric, salt, ginger and ground black pepper). Then add half the saffron. Put back on the heat and stir spices evenly (the chicken will start to look beautiful)

- Place the chicken onto a wire rack placed on a roasting tin. Cover the base of the roasting tin with a little water, then cover with a lid or tin foil. Put into oven on a high heat for 20 mins then turn down heat to 190°C. Roast for a further hour (this depends on the size of the chicken – 20 mins per 450g/1lb plus an extra 20 mins). Turn the chicken periodically during the cooking process

For the preserved lemon and olive sauce
- Place a drizzle of olive oil into a large pan then add the onion and garlic, stir until soft but don't allow to burn – approx 10 mins

- Next stir in the rest of the saffron, another pinch of salt, pepper, ginger and turmeric, add the water and simmer for approx 30 mins until reduced in volume

- Take chicken out of oven, arrange one of the preserved lemons over the chicken breast and re-cover with the lid/tin foil. Place on the side to rest

- Back to the sauce: put rest of the lemons and the olives into the sauce and gently simmer for 10 mins – at this stage you may want to add some of the chicken stock

- Add more spices if necessary

- Now cut chicken into portions and arrange with the sauce

> My mum is the Queen of the neighbourhood – she has always been well-respected and in charge in the community!
>
> This is a magic dish. When I was a little kid watching my mum cook I didn't realise I was learning at the same time. I love to cook but if I'm unsure about something I will call my mum and she will answer my problems. I don't think my cooking is as good as my mum's although my family and kids say it's really good.

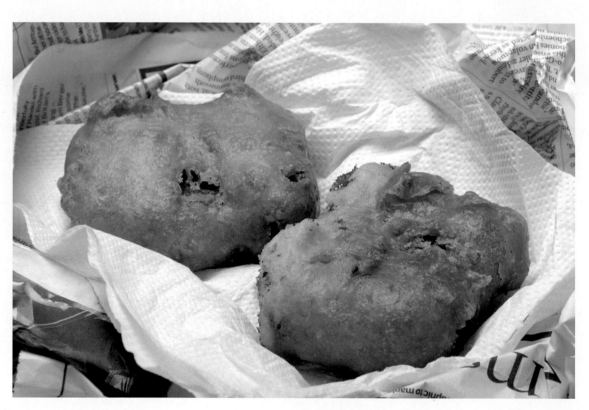

477 Kcals per average serving

The pattie in the sock with gravel lot

Makes 4–5 corned beef patties

Ingredients

1 tin corned beef – thickly sliced
Flour to coat

Batter

2 cups plain flour
1 egg – beaten
2 cups milk
Pinch of salt and pepper

Method

- To make the batter, put flour in a bowl, make a well, gradually add the milk, egg, salt and pepper
- Coat the corned beef slices with flour then dip into the batter
- Deep fry for approx 5 mins until golden brown in colour
- Drain well on kitchen paper

When I was 9 or 10 years old my family and I went camping to Whitton Castle in Whitton-le-Wear, for two weeks. The holiday went well at first but midway through the two weeks, I stayed out past the time I was supposed to.

My mam and dad came back with fish, chips and corn beef patties for us all (my two brothers, sister and me). During eating these, my mam and dad were told that I had stayed out later than I should have done, that's where the corn beef pattie comes into it. I put the pattie down my sock and ran away fearing a hiding from my dad. My sister always remembers this as, THE PATTIE IN THE SOCK.

I was about 11 or 12 years old and we all went camping again to Whitton Castle, I was a bit of a handful for my parents by that age. I had an argument with my dad, they said, 'We are going home,' and I ran off yet again.

There was a chip shop on the camp site and I went in as bold as brass and asked for chips and batter. However being the cheeky lad that I was I was thrown out or I was not served, so I picked up loads of gravel stones and threw them into the chip shop fryers. I was then heard shouting, 'Give me a gravel lot,' by my sister whilst running away laughing. My sister and my family always remember me when they eat fish and chips and batter and corn beef patties – which were served in newspaper.

Cawl – Welsh stew

Serves 4–6

Ingredients

2 onions – peeled and roughly chopped
4 medium sized potatoes – peeled and roughly chopped
4 medium sized carrots – peeled and roughly chopped
2 leeks – peeled and roughly chopped
½ medium sized swede – peeled and roughly chopped
2 garlic cloves – peeled, crushed and chopped
2 teaspoon chopped rosemary (fresh or dried)
2 teaspoon mustard seeds
2 tablespoons olive oil
900ml / 1½ pints vegetable stock
1.5kg / 3lb lamb leg joint
Pinch of salt and pepper

Method

- Lightly fry onions in olive oil in a large saucepan or cast iron casserole dish

- Add the lamb to colour, approx 8 mins

- Add the rest of the vegetables, garlic, rosemary and mustard seeds, brown for approx 8 mins

- Add stock to pan to clean all the lamb juices from bottom of the pan. If necessary move to bigger pan. Simmer for approx 1½ hours with lid on pan

- Carefully take the meat from the pan, remove from bone and cut into bite-sized chunks. Place the meat and bone back into pan for approx 1 hour with more stock if required

- Take the bone out of the pan. Season to taste

482 Kcals per average serving

> "This recipe originated from my mother who is Welsh. During war times, the mining communities did not have a great deal of money for food. Communities would share out food to create a communal broth. Families would share this Welsh broth between those with little money.
>
> I believe this recipe was passed down through generations; it was the only recipe that my mother taught me to cook. My mother said, 'As long as you make a good broth you'll have good friends.' "

> Growing up, I lived in Bangladesh with my family. Fish was our usual everyday food, and meat was eaten at special celebrations.
>
> The villagers and other people who knew there would be a special celebration would get together to eat. This would take place outside, sitting on the floor around long tables.
>
> Either a cow or two goats would be slaughtered for the event. Some people would then cook it for everyone else to eat and enjoy.
>
> I liked this because there was a nice atmosphere; it was good because it meant that poor people could eat a really enjoyable meal.

Bangladesh lamb curry

Serves 2–3

Ingredients

4 lamb chops
2 onions – peeled and chopped.
2 cloves garlic – crushed, peeled and chopped
2 tablespoons olive oil
New potatoes – 3 medium sized handfuls, washed
1 small red chilli – deseeded and chopped finely
1 teaspoon curry powder
1 teaspoon chilli powder
1 teaspoon coriander
1 teaspoon turmeric
1 teaspoon cumin
4 kaffir lime leaves – roughly chopped
1 small handful basil leaves – roughly chopped
2 dessertspoons tomato purée
1 beef stock cube
300ml / ½ pt cold water

Method

- Place lamb chops in a wok or large frying pan with olive oil
- Brown on both sides – about 3 mins on each side
- Add the onions, red chilli and garlic. Cook until soft, about 8–10 mins
- Stir in the spices, lime leaves and basil
- Sprinkle the stock cube into the pan and stir evenly
- Add the tomato puree, then the water
- Stir in the potatoes
- Add salt and pepper
- Simmer for about 45 mins, stirring occasionally

Serve with basmati rice

441 Kcals per average serving

Panag

Serves 2–4

Ingredients

1 350g tin of good quality corned beef
1 beef stock cube
4 medium carrots
2 medium onions
4–5 large potatoes
Drizzle of olive or vegetable oil
Pinch of salt and pepper to taste
1 teaspoon cornflour or gravy thickener
A small piece of mature Cheddar cheese – grated

Method

- Preheat oven to 180°C, 350°F, gas mark 4

- Divide the corned beef lengthways into six to eight slices

- Peel onions, then cut into slices

- Scrub carrots then cut into slices

- Peel then cut potatoes lengthways into slices (not too thick)

- Spread oil very thinly over the bottom of a heavy-based casserole dish. Cover with potato slices, followed by half the onions then half the carrots. Position half of the corned beef slices on top of these vegetables

- Repeat the layering – more potato slices followed by the rest of the onions, carrots and corned beef

- Top it all with a final layer of potato slices, making sure the vegetables underneath aren't visible. Pour over enough stock to very lightly cover the top potato layer

- Cover the casserole dish with a lid or foil, and then cook in the middle of the oven for one hour

- Remove the lid or foil, check the seasoning, then cook uncovered for another 20 mins or until the top layer of potatoes is browned (sprinkle cheese over top after 10 mins)

- Serve the dish on warmed plates using a slotted spoon, keeping back the gravy

- In a cup, cover one teaspoon of cornflour with a small amount of cold water. Stir this well then pour it into the panag gravy, or use gravy thickener. Stirring continuously, heat the gravy on the hob until it thickens, then pour it over the plated meal

My tip: This was served with a good green Savoy cabbage or kale — which was cheap back then. It's a cheap tasty meal fit for royalty!

503 Kcals per average serving

I grew up in a small mining town near Barnsley in the 1950s and 1960s.

Panag was a dish served to us as kids by my mother. It was cheap, easy to prepare and tasted absolutely beautiful. We didn't get it very often unfortunately. My dad was working as a miner, earning good money so we had a basic but varied diet. We tended to eat the same thing on the same day. So Monday would be 'tatty ash' a stew made from the leftovers from Sunday dinner and so on through the week. You knew what day it was by what was served up for dinner.

My dad left the pits when I was 13, and suddenly money became scarce as he struggled to find work. So, being cheap, Panag became a regular fixture of our weekly diet. Of course with the innocence of youth, we were over the moon getting more of what we liked, more often.

Just goes to show every cloud has a silver lining when you are 13. I still cook it every now and then just for old time's sake. ”

My casserole dish — hand crafted by me!"

Rustic Kashmiri curry

Serves 4

Ingredients

6 chicken portions – leg and drumstick portions (ideally boned, then roughly diced into bite-sized chunks – most butchers will do this)
1–2 green chillies – finely chopped
1 tablespoon Kashmiri basaar
3 onions – roughly chopped
6 garlic cloves – crushed, peeled and finely chopped
2 tablespoons clarified butter or olive oil
1 thumb-sized piece root ginger – peeled and finely chopped
4 large fresh tomatoes – finely chopped
2 green peppers – deseeded and finely chopped
Pinch of salt and pepper
½ teaspoon dried methi (fenugreek)
1 large handful of fresh coriander – roughly chopped
½ teaspoon paprika
¼ teaspoon ground garam masala
1 cup cold water

Method

- Place the onion in a large saucepan with the clarified butter or olive oil. Gently fry on a medium heat until the onion is soft but not brown – approx 10 mins

- Add the chilli and stir for 5 mins

- Turn the heat up slightly and add the tomatoes, ginger, garlic and green peppers and cook for approx 10–15 mins – you will see the juices start to reduce

- Next add the basaar and stir for 5 mins

- Add the chicken pieces and stir well

- Now add the water and cook for about 10 mins – you will need to stir continuously at this stage to stop the ingredients from sticking

- Turn back to medium heat and simmer for 10 mins. Add paprika then add garam masala, methi, black pepper and coriander

My tip: Serve with Keza's special rice

569 Kcals per serving

I love my mum's cooking. Over the last few years my mum's style of cooking has motivated me to want to cook like her. This has motivated me to progress and get better.

When I was on the assessment ward I started to understand the importance of family support and family connections in helping me in my recovery.

My mum has passed on her cookery knowledge, love and support, but I wouldn't have developed and gained the confidence without the support of the staff – especially my Occupational Therapist Assistant (Keza). During the Eid period I cooked this curry for the whole of the hospital, people loved it! It was a huge confidence booster but very scary!!

Keza's Story

At one stage we were quite limited in what we could do together because there was no access to knives and sharp tools.

I wanted to start to develop a therapeutic relationship with this person, and found that we could connect by talking about food and learning about the cultural background. We both shared an interest in food and family.

I have learnt so much about different food and cultures. My family are very pleased that I know how to cook a typical Asian curry and rice – I've got this particular patient to thank for that!

Keza's special rice

Ingredients

2 large cups basmati rice – white or brown
1 onion – roughly chopped
2 clove garlic – crushed, peeled and roughly chopped
1 dessertspoon olive oil
1 large handful mixed spices in their whole state (garam masala – you can buy this in packets)
Water to cover

Method

- Soak the rice in cold water for about 30 mins. Then using a sieve drain, rinse and drain again

- Put the olive oil in a medium sized saucepan with the onion, garlic and garam masala. Cook out the spices for about 10 mins. Cool slightly

- Next carefully add the water – enough to cover half the saucepan

- Drain through the sieve, discard the onion, garlic and spices but keep the stock. Transfer the stock back into the saucepan and add the rice and a pinch of salt

- Put back onto the heat and gently simmer with lid on until rice is soft and the liquid has evaporated – approx 10 mins. The rice will become brown in appearance

Puddings
& Desserts

Chocolate cake with silver 'ball bearings'

Serves 8–10

Ingredients

150g / 6oz self raising flour
150g / 6oz butter/margarine
150g / 6oz sugar
3 eggs – beaten
25g / 1oz cocoa powder
25g / 1oz melted chocolate – milk or dark

To fill and decorate

300ml / 10fl oz carton double cream

1 small bar milk or plain chocolate – melted

Silver candy balls or hundreds and thousands

Method

- Preheat oven to 180⁰C, 350⁰F, gas mark 4
- Beat together fat and sugar until light and fluffy in appearance
- Gradually stir in the beaten egg mixture
- Carefully fold in the flour and cocoa powder then stir in the melted chocolate
- Transfer to an 8 inch (20 cm) round or square cake tin, lined with greased tin foil or baking parchment
- Place in the oven for approx 25–30 mins until the sponge springs back when touched with your forefinger
- Cool and remove from the tin
- Carefully peel the foil/parchment from the sponge then cut the sponge in half
- In a large bowl, whisk the cream lightly
- Sandwich the sponge together with the whipped cream. Carefully decorate the top of the cake with the melted chocolate and the silver candy balls/hundreds and thousands

My tip: Serve with a nice cup of tea!

415 Kcals per average slice

"

I come from a large family where I was the eldest of nine sisters and two brothers. Every Sunday afternoon my mum would visit my grandma and take two of the children with her. My mum would do this fairly so we all got the chance to see my grandma.

We loved it at Grandma's house; she would always make a cake. My favourite was a chocolate cake decorated with silver 'ball bearings', which she served on a china plate with a blue pattern around the rim.

If it was nice weather we would sit outside; I remember seeing lots of ants outside and my grandad would be at the top of the garden in his shed. "

Blackberry and apple crumble

Serves 6–8

Ingredients

For the filling

1kg / 2lb 4oz Bramley apples
400g / 1lb blackberries
2 tablespoons Demerara sugar
2 lemons

For the topping

250g / 10oz plain flour
150g / 5oz butter
150g / 5oz Demerara sugar
100g / 4oz mixed oats, seeds, chopped nuts (muesli mixture)

Method

- Preheat the oven to 190⁰C, 375⁰F, gas mark 5
- Peel, core and chop apples into chunks
- Squeeze lemon juice over apples and mix well
- Layer apples, sugar and blackberries in a large ovenproof dish
- Put flour in a large bowl, add sugar
- Rub in butter until mixture looks like breadcrumbs
- Add the muesli mixture and mix well
- Sprinkle the crumble mixture over the fruit mixture
- Bake for 30–45 mins until top is golden in appearance

338 Kcals per average serving

When I was younger my grandma used to look after me and my brother when my mum went to work.

One thing I remember vividly is when my grandma used to take us blackberry picking. We would pick loads of blackberries from the countryside and would get Bramley apples from an allotment close to where Grandma lived.

We would take this fruit back to Grandma's house where she would make the most gorgeous fruit crumble.

Fairy cakes

Makes 12

100g / 4oz caster sugar
100g / 4oz margarine
2 eggs
100g / 4 oz self-raising flour

For the butter icing

100g / 4oz butter
200g / 8oz caster sugar
Few drops of food colouring and/or flavouring (optional)

Method

- Preheat the oven 180°C, 350°F, gas mark 4
- Line cupcake tray with 12 cupcake cases
- Cream together the caster sugar and the margarine in a mixing bowl
- Add the eggs one at a time and beat after each addition
- Sift in the flour gradually, and fold in
- Divide the cake mixture between the cake cases and bake in the oven for 15–20 mins, until a cake tester (or cocktail stick) placed into one of the cakes comes out clean
- Leave to cool for at least 20 mins

To make the butter icing

- Beat butter and sugar together until it has gone paler in colour
- Add any colourings and flavourings and beat in
- Spread or pipe the icing onto the cakes as desired

280 Kcals per fairy cake

> I remember throughout my childhood having these wonderful, elaborate birthday cakes every year – my grandma would make the cake and shape it and my mum would decorate it.
>
> It was my mum, though, who taught me this simple ratio and method for baking a sponge cake – she always uses butter icing made with caster sugar without weighing, adding the ingredients until it 'looks right'.
>
> I have used the basic recipe in numerous shapes and sizes over the years but my current favourite is fairy cakes with coloured icing piped on to the top.

> *I used to love baking with my mum when I was younger. My mum taught me how to make lots of things which I still do to this day – I would say I am a better baker than my mum now!*
>
> *This recipe takes me back to Christmas time when me and my mum would make this as an alternative to Christmas cake. It is a very indulgent cake and it was always centre of attention, bringing back memories of happy times – Christmas and family togetherness. We would eat this at teatime and my dad would cut the cake – giving himself the first and biggest piece: 'cutter's perks' he would say.*
>
> *When I became unwell I went to live back home again. It was a very difficult time for me and my family. We had no experience of mental health problems in our family. In the beginning, my mum and dad didn't know how to care for me – they took on the role of looking after a little girl again. They thought it was their fault and soon came to realise that they couldn't put a sticking plaster over my illness.*
>
> *I became more isolated. One day my mum gently talked me in to helping her bake, asking me what I would like to make – chocolate cake of course!*
>
> *From that day on, bit by bit I started to feel better in myself. Baking with my mum helped me, and helped my mum to understand certain problems I was going through. We would chat and bake at the same time. Baking distracted me from other issues. I felt safe – in a warm, familiar environment.*

Festive chocolate cake

Serves 8–10

Ingredients

150g / 6oz self-raising flour
150g / 6oz butter or margarine
150g / 6oz caster sugar
3 eggs
1 tablespoon cocoa powder
50g / 2oz bar dark chocolate – melted

To decorate

1 200g / 8oz bar milk chocolate – melted
1 small jar Nutella™ chocolate spread
Small bag Maltesers™ – roughly crushed
Chocolate buttons – large or small

Method

- Preheat the oven to 180°C 350°F, gas mark 4
- Use a 6 inch (15 cm) square or round cake tin: grease the tin and line the bottom with greaseproof paper or parchment paper
- Cream the butter and sugar together in a large bowl – either by hand with a wooden spoon or by electric whisk/mixer – until light and fluffy in appearance
- In a separate bowl mix together the flour and cocoa powder
- In another bowl lightly beat the eggs together
- Now gradually fold half the flour and eggs into the sugar/butter mixture, then fold in the other half until evenly mixed
- Fold the melted dark chocolate into the cake mixture
- Carefully transfer into the prepared cake tin and spread evenly
- Place in the oven, top shelf, for approximately 25–30 mins. Test for 'doneness' at the 25 mins stage by placing a skewer into the cake. If the cake is ready the skewer will be clean with no signs of sponge residue
- Cool slightly. then transfer onto a cooling tray

To decorate

- When cold, carefully cut through the middle of the cake and spread Nutella™ evenly on the bottom half
- Sandwich the halves together, then spread the melted milk chocolate all over the cake and decorate with buttons and Maltesers™

434 Kcals per average slice

These special angels symbolise
my children

Nana's bread and butter pudding

Serves 4–5

Ingredients

6 slices of bread – buttered
75g / 3 oz Demerara sugar
2 tablespoons mixed dried fruit (e.g. sultanas, raisins, cranberries)
1 orange – juice
2 large eggs
Large mug of whole milk

Method

- Preheat the oven to 150⁰C, 300⁰F, gas mark 2
- Line an ovenproof dish with slices of bread and butter cut into triangles
- Add a good sprinkle of sugar, mixed dried fruit and some freshly squeezed orange
- Continue to layer in this way. Put a layer of bread and butter on top
- Beat the eggs with the milk and pour over the top
- Sprinkle with more sugar. Bake for 1 hour

My tips:

— I like to use seeded batch or good wholemeal bread to give the pudding more texture

— You may need to adjust the amount of milk and eggs depending on the size of the pudding to ensure all the bread is covered

— This pudding is delicious served with cream, ice cream or custard

241 Kcals per average serving

"Remember, practice makes perfect. Happy baking from Nana."

> Nana loved home cooking, giving nourishment and comfort to her husband, 5 children and 14 grandchildren. She had a very sweet tooth and particularly liked her puddings.
>
> She passed away at the ripe old age of 87 in 2004 and was survived by Grandad who lived to 89. They ate a good healthy range of fruit and vegetables long before 5-a-day came along.
>
> It is lovely that her memory lives on in her recipes for her great-grandchildren to enjoy.

Banana loaf

Makes 1 loaf serving 8–10 slices

Ingredients

100g / 4oz butter
100g / 4oz light muscovado sugar
2 large ripe bananas – mashed
3 large eggs – lightly whisked
100g / 4oz white self-raising flour
25g / 1oz wholemeal self-raising flour
50g / 2oz porridge oats
1 dessertspoon olive oil
2 small handfuls of sultanas

Method

- Preheat the oven to 180ºC, 350ºF, gas mark 4
- Line a 2lb (900g) loaf tin with a cake liner or greaseproof paper
- Cream the butter and sugar together until light and creamy in colour and texture
- Add the mashed bananas and stir well
- Gradually add the eggs
- Fold in the two types of flour, porridge oats and sultanas
- Then fold in the olive oil
- Transfer evenly to the prepared loaf tin
- Place in the preheated oven for approx 35 mins. (Test with a cake skewer: place the skewer in the middle of the cake – if it comes away clean then the cake is done)
- Cool slightly, then transfer onto a cooling tray

My tip: Add 1 teaspoon of your favourite spice to add more flavour — I like cinnamon

182 Kcals per average slice

> From an early age I lived in two children's homes.
>
> In one of the homes we had banana loaf once a week. I can still remember the smell of the loaf baking in the oven. Banana loaf was a popular pudding amongst the children.
>
> The unit was only small and there were between 10 and 12 children living there. I remember feeling safe and secure, and how nice the staff were – I was often called a 'cheeky monkey'.
>
> I look back at my time spent in these two homes with great fondness and happiness; they have been the best time in my life so far.

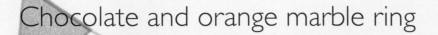

Chocolate and orange marble ring

Serves 10–12 (based on a 8 inch/20 cm ring tin)

Ingredients

200g / 8oz self-raising flour
200g / 8oz butter – softened
200g / 8oz golden granulated sugar
4 medium sized eggs – beaten
2 large juicy oranges – grated rind and juice
1 dessertspoon cocoa
50g / 2oz or 8 pieces of good quality milk or dark
chocolate – melted

Method

- Preheat the oven to 180°C, 350°F, gas mark 4

- Lightly grease an 8 inch (20 cm) cake tin

- Cream the butter and sugar together until light
  and fluffy

- Gradually mix in the eggs

- Fold in the flour

- Using an additional bowl, separate the cake
  mixture into 2 equal parts

- In the first bowl stir in the cocoa powder and
  the melted chocolate

- In the second bowl stir in the orange juice and
  rind

- Now start to transfer the cake mixture into
  the tin. Using a tablespoon, place an alternate
  spoonful of the cake mixtures in the tin. Repeat
  this process a second time. Using a cake skewer
  make swirling actions through the cake

- Place in the oven for about 25–30 mins. Test the
  cake for 'doneness' by placing the cake skewer
  in the cake – if it comes out clean it is done

- Cool slightly and transfer onto a cooling rack.
  When cold place on a serving plate or place on a
  cake stand

My tip: You can make this cake in a round,
square, ring or loaf tin

298 Kcals per average slice

> "
> After many years of abuse I was taken
> into foster care. My foster parents lived
> in a large six-bedroomed house with
> three children of their own plus other
> foster children.
>
> I felt that I fitted in, and soon became
> part of the family. After a short while I
> began to call my foster parents Mum and
> Dad. My mum said I was as much her
> child as the rest of her children.
>
> My mum was a special lady. She was a
> very positive influence in my life – she
> made me feel safe, and had a great
> sense of humour.
>
> Every birthday I remember my mum
> making me a marble cake. This marble
> cake was all the colours of the rainbow
> and highly flavoured with chocolate,
> peppermint, strawberry etc. The cake
> seemed to me to represent my mum's
> huge personality.
>
> As I have got older I have adapted the
> cake recipe to more subtle colours and
> flavours. Whilst in hospittal I have raised
> over £100 for a charity by making cakes,
> including the marble cake.
>
> Sadly my mum passed away, but I still
> keep in touch with the rest of the family.
> My mum has kept her legacy alive
> through her children, who offer support,
> warmth and love. "

Mixed fruit crumble

Serves 4–5

Ingredients

Crumble mix
100g / 4oz plain or self-raising flour
50g / 2oz butter or margarine
75g / 3oz sugar
1 Weetabix or handful of porridge oats

Or cheat and buy a crumble mix from your supermarket!

Fruits
450g / 1lb of fruit:
Apples (preferably cooking apples but eating apples will do) – peeled and cored
Rhubarb (if you like it) 4 or more sticks
Plus handfuls of any of the following:
• Cherries
• Gooseberries
• Plums
• Blueberries
• Redcurrants
• Raspberries
• Grapes
• Strawberries
• Blackberries
• Raisins – use raisins instead of sugar in your fruit mix – far healthier!
White sugar – 2 tablespoons, or to taste

Method

Fruits
• Wash all your fruits and cut them up if necessary. If using grapes or berries leave them whole. Don't forget to take the stones out of any cherries, plums etc

• Place the uncooked fruit in an ovenproof dish. Add a little white sugar – 2 tablespoons (depending on sweet or sharp you like your fruit) – or add a handful of raisins instead of sugar

Crumble mix
• Preheat the oven to 190ºC, 375ºF, gas mark 5

• Sieve the flour and rub the butter into it. Add the sugar and mix in

• Sprinkle the crumbs evenly over the fruit

• Sprinkle a Weetabix or oats on the top of the crumble for extra crunch

• Bake in a moderate oven for approximately 30–40 mins until the crumble is golden brown

• If you need to reheat later on, just place a portion in a dish and put in the microwave for 1 minute

My tips: The recipe for this crumble is simple and flexible, using whatever fruit you may have readily available – I hope you give it a try and enjoy it, as I did as a child and still do today

Enjoy on its own or with custard, cream or ice cream

267 Kcals per average serving

My map of Somerset

> " My childhood memories are rich with growing up in a small village in a rural part of Somerset – a beautiful place.
>
> Food wise, my key memories are of thrift, community spirit and sharing.
>
> We all took advantage of local food that was grown in our own gardens, allotments and fields, or could be found growing wild in the countryside.
>
> I have great memories of summers – in particular, being taken on long family walks on hot sunny days, down picturesque lanes with tall hedges, across fields and through woods and orchards, picking wild gooseberries, strawberries, blackberries and many other fruits.
>
> Neighbours with fruit trees had an abundance of fruit which they would share with others in the village – apples, plums, pears and other such fruits.
>
> For Sunday lunch, for pudding we would have homemade crumble, filled with whatever fruit we had to hand. "

B's banana bonanza

Serves 1–2

Ingredients

1 banana – skin left on
10 chocolate buttons

Method

- Preheat the oven to 200⁰C, 400⁰F, gas mark 6
- Make five incisions into the banana – big enough to place the chocolate buttons inside
- Put buttons into the slits until you can't see them anymore
- Wrap in tin foil and bake in oven for 15–20 mins
- Cool slightly, then cut at angles into small pieces
- Arrange on a plate and serve

My tips:

— As an alternative to baking in the oven try BBQ-ing

— As an alternative to chocolate buttons, try raisins instead

— For an ice-lolly experience: take 1 banana, peel and chop in half. Place a lolly stick in each half and transfer to the freezer. Leave to freeze then serve — this tastes so good, and you won't believe you are eating something so healthy

190 Kcals per serving

> *A couple of years ago I joined 'Weight Watchers' and managed to lose eight stone.*
>
> *This recipe is one that I adapted to satisfy a craving for something sweet, filling and partly nutritious at the end of the day. It brings back fond memories, because in the group it became my signature dish.*

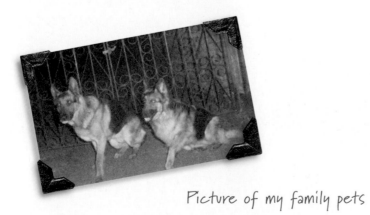

Picture of my family pets

Rice pudding

Serves 4

Ingredients

75g / 3oz short grain (pudding) rice
1 tablespoon sugar – white or brown
A few drops of vanilla essence or extract
900ml / 1½ pints semi-skimmed milk
Grated nutmeg
A little butter to grease the oven proof dish

Method

- Preheat the oven to 160°C, 325°F, gas mark 3
- Grease the ovenproof dish with the butter
- Place the rice into the dish then cover with the milk. Stir in the vanilla and sugar. Mix well. Grate as much or as little nutmeg over the top as you like
- Put in oven for about 2 hours. Stir periodically

My tip: Depending how runny you like your rice pudding, add more milk during the baking process if necessary

212 Kcals per serving

> "
> *My earliest recollection of eating my mum's rice pudding was when I was about 7 years old. We usually had rice pudding at the weekend when my mum used to bake.*
>
> *I was the youngest of three children and was always allowed to have the skin in addition to a bowlful of rice pudding.*
>
> *I remember at meal times we would sit round the dining room table together – this was when my mum and dad had a really good chat to us.*
>
> *I miss my family and the family changes. I can understand why my predicament has broken down my family unit.*
>
> *I used to enjoy eating anything that my mum prepared. I think of happy times with my family when I'm feeling low. I still remember the smell of the rice pudding baking in the oven – when I used to play outside, you could smell my mum's cooking down the street!!*
> "

Auntie Mickey's cheesecake

Serves 8–10

You require an 8 inch (20 cm) square or circular loose bottom cake tin, greased with oil or butter

Ingredients

For the filling and topping

450g / 1lb of curd cheese (or cream cheese)
2 eggs – beaten
1 cup of caster sugar
1 tablespoon self-raising flour (sieved)
Approximately 2 tablespoons single cream
2 x 300ml / 10fl oz cartons of sour cream
1 dessertspoon caster sugar (for the topping)
2 teaspoons vanilla extract

For the base

200g / 8oz digestive biscuits
2 level tablespoons golden syrup
2 level tablespoons cocoa
50g / 2oz butter (salted or unsalted)

My tip: As an alternative for the base, try using 4 small sponge cakes made into crumbs, instead of the digestive biscuits

423 Kcals per average serving

Try using low fat cottage cheese instead of cream cheese, reducing the calorie content to 245 Kcals per average serving

Method

- Preheat oven to 160ºC, 325ºF, gas mark 3

To make the base

- Crush biscuits (put in a plastic bag and roll with a rolling pin)
- Heat golden syrup, butter and cocoa in a saucepan until it is a loose syrup consistency. Take off the heat and add the biscuit crumbs
- Stir thoroughly and then spoon into the base of the prepared tin

To make the filling

- Mix the curd or cream cheese and sugar by hand with a wooden spoon or spatula
- Add the beaten eggs one at a time. Then add the single cream – a tablespoon at a time until the mixture reaches a soft but not runny consistency
- Next add the self-raising flour and finally the vanilla essence
- Mix this all well and then place in the cake tin on top of the biscuit base
- Bake for 30 minutes at the bottom of the oven

While the cheesecake is cooking

- Mix the sour cream with a dessertspoon of sugar
- At the end of 30 minutes take the cake out and spread the sour cream mix onto the top of the cake
- Put back in the oven for 5 minutes and then remove
- Allow to cool in a cool place for several hours and then put into the fridge
- When ready to serve, carefully remove from tin

My tips: The cheesecake may be frozen and will keep for several months, although it may be slightly more granular when it has been frozen and defrosted.

A small slice per person is usually enough as the cake is very rich

> My mother was the eldest of five children born in the East End of London. Her next youngest sister – my Aunt Miriam (or Mickey) who has celebrated her 99th birthday this year and lived on her own until 96 – was a truly excellent cook.
>
> She had many signature dishes but my two favourites were a wonderful chocolate soufflé which was as light as a feather and an even more wonderful cheesecake. I learnt her cheesecake recipe many years ago. It is one of the few dishes I cook and one that is enjoyed by everyone who tastes it – and was in fact my daughter's favourite for a birthday cake.
>
> Over the years I have experimented a bit with the recipe, finding the addition of real vanilla essence gives the cake a wonderful flavour.
>
> Some years ago I discovered I was gluten intolerant and I found a way to make the cake gluten free. The cake as originally made is very high in calories and so I have also made a lower carbohydrate version. (Note: not really low carb, just lower – see page 188 for the recipe)

Malt loaf

Makes 1 loaf serving 8–10 slices

Ingredients

One mug of each:

Bran cereal e.g. All Bran™
Sultanas
Sugar
Milk
Self-raising flour

Method

- Preheat the oven to 190ºC, 375ºF, gas mark 5
- Mix the cereal, sultanas, sugar and milk together and allow to stand for one hour
- Mix in the self-raising flour
- Grease and line a 2lb (900g) loaf tin with greaseproof paper, put cake mixture into tin and bake for approx 45 mins to one hour
- Test with a knife or knitting needle to see if it is cooked

132 Kcals per average slice

> " My dad used to make this with us as children as it is such an easy recipe to follow. It was one of the first cakes we made as children and I still make it now.
>
> The malt loaf was one of the first cakes I ever made because it is so easy to make and doesn't require lots of stirring. "

Boobelach

Boobelach is a Jewish recipe. These sweet dumplings are coated in cinnamon for extra taste.

Makes 6

Ingredients

3 eggs
1 cup of water
1/2 teaspoon salt
100g / 4oz fine matzo meal
Vegetable/sunflower oil for frying
1 dessertspoon granulated sugar and 1 teaspoon cinnamon – mixed together

Method

- Beat together the eggs, water and salt in a medium sized bowl
- Gradually add the matzo meal to make a thick batter – add more if necessary
- Form the mixture into balls or patties
- Shallow fry in the oil until golden brown – about 4 mins either side
- Drain on kitchen paper and dust with the sugar and cinnamon mixture

My tip: Coat your hands with matzo meal before rolling the mixture into balls/patties to prevent sticking

212 Kcals per serving

> *I am and always have been a family oriented person. When I was a little girl, my grandmother was the hub of our family. Her name was Rebecca but she was affectionately known as Bubbe by her grandchildren. Every weekend all my aunties, uncles and cousins would go to Bubbe's house for a get-together and a meal.*
>
> *Celebratory events such as the Jewish New Year (September) would be held at Bubbe's house. We would always have Boobelach on such occasions. I remember helping to take them to the table and I remember the fragrant smell of cinnamon was too hard to resist so I would have a nibble before they reached the table! My family mean so much to me. Since my husband was diagnosed as bipolar my family have been extremely supportive and understanding.*

This tea set is very special
to me. The Hollyhock flowers
remind me of when my
grandparents set up a small
flower garden at their house
for me to look after."

> "
>
> At the age of 17 I became a mother. I didn't have any family support so I was taken into care in a mother and baby unit. If it wasn't for this unit I would never have got my life sorted out.
>
> Whenever I felt particularly low in this unit, there was a cook who would try and cheer me up. She used to make this amazing pineapple upside down cake which became known in the unit as 'depression cake'. When I ate this cake it made me feel good about myself – as if it had some special magic in it. The weight was instantly lifted off my shoulders – it was brilliant!
>
> Other people in the unit started to ask the cook to make depression cake – she would say, 'See what you've started now!'
>
> "

'Depression cake' – pineapple upside down cake

Serves 6–8

Ingredients

150g / 6oz self-raising flour
150g / 6oz butter – softened
150g / 6oz caster sugar
25g / 1oz ground almonds (optional)
3 medium sized eggs – beaten
1 tablespoon milk
A few drops vanilla extract
Small handful glace cherries
1 large tin pineapple rings (use approx 8) or use fresh pineapple – peeled and sliced into rings

Method

- Preheat the oven to 180°C, 325°F, gas mark 4

- Cream the sugar and butter together by hand or by using a mixer

- Gradually add the beaten egg, mix until evenly distributed

- Now carefully fold in the flour and ground almonds (if using)

- Mix in the milk and vanilla extract

- Grease a medium sized baking tin or medium sized ovenproof dish then neatly arrange the pineapple over the base

- Place a glace cherry in the centre of each pineapple ring

- Now carefully spoon the cake mixture over the top, then smooth evenly

- Place in the oven for approx 30 mins until light golden in appearance and the sponge springs back when touched

- Leave to cool, then turn out

My tip: Try this homemade cake – shop bought is not the same!

408 Kcals per average serving

Gran's treacle tart

Serves 6

Ingredients

For the shortcrust pastry
225g / 8oz plain flour
100g / 4oz butter, softened at room temperature
1 tablespoon of water

For the filling
8–9 tablespoons golden syrup
3 tablespoons fresh breadcrumbs
1 lemon – grated zest and juice

Method

- Preheat oven to 180°C, 325°F, gas mark 4
- To make the pastry, place the flour in a large bowl and add the butter
- Using your fingertips, rub the butter into the flour until the mixture resembles fine breadcrumbs
- Gradually add the water and mix together using a knife, until it forms a soft dough
- Place the dough on a clean, floured surface and roll out as thinly as possible
- Carefully transfer the rolled out pastry into a large tart tin or ovenproof tart/ flan dish. Trim off excess pastry and put to one side
- In another bowl, put golden syrup, breadcrumbs, lemon zest and juice together and stir until evenly distributed. Carefully spread over the lined pastry case
- Roll out spare pastry, cut into thin strips and decorate the tart as desired
- Place in the oven for approx 30 mins until filling is a rich golden colour

417 Kcals per serving

" I learnt to bake from my gran. She made each of her grandchildren their own baking apron and we had our own special baking table. Baking with Gran was a nice treat – my mum didn't cook, she used to burn everything!

I especially remember making our own treacle tarts with our names made out of pastry.

Thinking about the treacle tarts brings back happy memories of being with Gran, baking and feeling safe and secure in her warm house with a comforting coal fire. "

Extra Things

Auntie Mickey's cheesecake: gluten free and lower sugar version

Serves 8–10

"The trickiest part for this version of the cheesecake is the base. I have so far come up with two alternatives and am experimenting with a third."

Ingredients

For the base

Either buy a gluten free ginger or honey cake, cut thick slices and place them in the base of the cake tin

or

Use a low sugar, gluten free brownie mix (Dixie Diners™ is one commercially available) plus
50g / 2ozs of unsweetened chocolate
50g / 2oz butter
2 eggs

For the filling and topping

450g / 1lb curd cheese or cream cheese
½ cup artificial sweetener e.g. Canderel™
1 tablespoon soy flour plus 1 teaspoon baking powder or use 1 tablespoon gluten free self-raising flour (Doves Farm™ or other)
2 eggs
2 tablespoons single cream
2 teaspoons vanilla extract
2 x 300ml / 10fl oz cartons sour cream
½ dessertspoon of artificial sweetener e.g. Canderel™

Method

- Preheat oven to 160°C, 325°F, gas mark 3

To make the base

- Grease an 8 inch (20 cm) square or circular loose bottom cake tin
- Mix the brownie mix with the other ingredients. Cook, put into the cake tin and allow to cool

To make the filling

- Mix curd cheese, sweetener, flour and baking powder (or self-raising flour), 2 beaten eggs (one at a time), single cream and the vanilla extract. Mix together and place onto the base of the loose bottom cake tin
- Bake for approx 30 minutes then add the topping (a mix of the sour cream and sweetener)
- Bake for a further 5 minutes before removing, allow to cool and then refrigerate
- Carefully remove the cheesecake from the tin when cold

Sage and onion stuffing

Ingredients

1 large onion – peeled and finely chopped
1 large handful of fresh sage – roughly chopped
Pinch of salt and pepper
75g / 3oz fresh wholemeal breadcrumbs
1 tablespoon olive oil
1 small egg – beaten

Method

- Preheat oven to 190°C, 375°F, gas mark 5
- Sauté the onion in the olive oil in a medium sized saucepan until soft – 5–8 mins
- Stir in the sage, then the breadcrumbs. Cook for about 5 mins, stirring occasionally
- Take off the heat, cool slightly then stir in the beaten egg, and season
- Transfer into a greased ovenproof dish or tin and bake for about 10–15 mins until slightly golden in appearance

Pease pudding recipe

(from rustic pea and ham soup see page 43)

Ingredients

225g / 9oz split peas – soaked overnight in cold water, then drained
A knob of butter
1 egg – beaten
Pinch of salt and pepper

Method

- Put the peas in a clean tea towel and fasten with string. Place in a large saucepan. Cover with cold water and boil gently for about 2–2 ½ hours – until the peas are tender
- Remove the peas from the tea towel. Using a wooden spoon, push through a sieve into a large bowl
- Mix in the butter, egg and salt and pepper

Dumplings

Ingredients

2 cups self-raising flour
Pinch of salt
Pinch of sugar
Cold water
Olive oil (to shallow fry) or a pan of boiling water

Method

- Place all the dry ingredients in a bowl and stir in enough cold water to form a soft dough

- To cook: either shallow fry in the olive oil (3 mins either side) or poach in the boiling water (6 mins). Drain well and serve

Rice and peas

Ingredients

1 medium sized onion – chopped finely
1 small handful of fresh thyme – roughly chopped
2 cupfuls of long grain rice
225ml / 8fl oz pint coconut milk
200g / 8oz cow peas
300ml / ½ pint water
1 dessertspoon olive oil
Pinch of salt and pepper

Method

- Gently sauté the onion in the olive oil until soft but not coloured – 6 mins

- Stir in the rice, then add the coconut milk and water

- Stir in the thyme, cow peas, salt and pepper and simmer gently for about 10–15 mins until the rice is just cooked and the liquid almost evaporated

- Stir regularly – you may need to add more water in the early stages

Yorkshire pudding

Makes 12 individual puddings

Ingredients

1½ cups plain flour
300ml / ½ pint cold milk
Pinch of salt and pepper
3 medium sized eggs
2 tablespoons olive oil

Method

- Whisk eggs in a small bowl or measuring jug
- Gradually add the flour, beat until smooth
- Gradually add the milk until mixture looks like a smooth batter
- Add salt and pepper
- Rest in the fridge for about 30 mins
- Pour olive oil evenly into 12-holed Yorkshire pudding / muffin tin
- Place in oven for about 5–8 mins until hot
- Carefully take out of oven and pour the batter equally into each hole
- Place in oven for approx 20–25 mins, until well risen, golden in colour and crisp in texture

Conversion charts

An approximate guide to metric and imperial measurements

Oven temperatures

	Gas	Fahrenheit (°F)	Celsius (°C)
Low/slow	1	275	140
	2	300	150
Moderate	3	325	160
	4	350	180
Fairly hot	5	375	190
	6	400	200
High/hot	7	425	220
	8	450	230
Very hot	9	475	240
	10	500	260

Weights

Imperial	Metric
½ oz	15g
1oz	25g
2oz	50g
3oz	75g
4oz (¼ lb)	100g
5oz	150g
6oz	175g
7oz	200g
8oz (½ lb)	225g (approx ¼ kg)
12oz (¾ lb)	350g
16oz (1lb)	450g (approx ½ kg)

Measures

Imperial	Metric
1 teaspoon (tsp)	5ml
1 tablespoon (tbsp)	15ml
5 fl oz (¼ pint)	150ml
10 fl oz (½ pint)	300ml
15 fl oz (¾ pint)	425ml
20 fl oz (1 pint)	600ml

"I have enjoyed taking part, good communication and interaction with group members"

"Talking brought up lots of feelings — thought provoking"

"Listening to other people's life stories made me realise how personal food is to everybody"

"It has made me think about healthy eating as well as being confident that I'm now able to cook using my mum's recipe and that it tastes the same"

"Emotional: for me, like many people, life hasn't been a bed of roses. However, it's mainly the good memories that this project has evoked"

"I helped with another person's recipe"

More thoughts and feelings

of the people involved with this project

"I am more aware of the harm too much fatty food can do to us"

"This was a lovely project and very therapeutic"

"Talking about food brought back a past memory that made me feel warm inside"

"It has reminded me that I can cook and I will use this in the future to make healthier choices"

"It was a good experience of a period in my life when I worked in a job that I loved and it was nice to remember"

"I feel more confident to make meals on my own in the future — which hasn't always been the case"

Where the recipes come from

Glossary and interesting stuff

Ackee – is a small yellow fruit/vegetable which is soft in texture and has a semi-sweet taste. It's traditionally used in Caribbean cooking – you would normally serve this with salt fish or fried dumplings

Al dente – to cook something like noodles or pasta until just done – still firm in the middle

Atta – fine textured wholemeal flour mixed with milk or water to form dough to make flat bread such as chapattis

'Ball bearings' – this is what I used to call silver candy (cake decoration) balls when I was a child

Banana crispy samosa (pudding) – a normal samosa but when you bite into it the banana explodes in your mouth with loads of sugar, it's like a banana and syrup sauce, lovely!

Banana sarnie – a sandwich made with bananas

Banjo – a Sheffield term for a sandwich mainly consisting of bacon and egg

Basaar – is made up of a range of spices, e.g. curry powder, chilli powder, cumin powder, tomato powder, coriander powder. Before, you had to buy all these separately and mix them yourself, whereas now you can buy it mixed up from shops. You can choose a packet of mild basaar or hot basaar according to your own taste

Basmati rice – a type of long grain rice, usually used in savoury dishes

Battered crab sticks – crab sticks dipped in chip shop batter mix and fried in the deep fat fryer

Battered Mars™ bars – Mars™ bars dipped in chip shop batter mix and fried in the deep fat fryer

Black-eyed peas – is another name for cow peas

Blind scouse – a stew from Liverpool, which contains vegetables but no meat

Bockwurst – traditional German boiled sausages

Bell peppers – a small colourful variety of the sweet pepper

Bombek – Slovenian dressing made by mixing equal parts of pumpkin oil and olive oil with dried mustard and cider vinegar. Use on a mixed salad comprised of lettuce, boiled, cold new potatoes and sliced Spanish onion

Borosil dish – A glass ovenproof dish similar to Pyrex in appearance

Bratwurst – traditional German grilled sausages

Bread cake – a South Yorkshire word for bread roll/bun

Buckshee – this means 'free', but to me it means second helpings

Cardamom – an aromatic spice which can be used in sweet and savoury dishes

Carnivals – Black History Month usually happens in July. This is when we have carnivals to celebrate our ethnicity. What is good about carnivals is that you can go to any one of them and still have the same good quality food

Cauldron – a big pot/pan ideal for making large batches of soup

Chapatti – typical unleavened Indian bread

Chip/bacon buttie – is a sandwich made with bread and chips or bacon which originated in the North of England

Chocolate crunch – affectionately known as concrete at school and always served with pink custard

Clarified butter – is achieved by melting butter until the clear butter separates from the cloudy butter. You use the clear butter and discard the cloudy butter

Cob – is a bread roll

Coutlette – this is what I call a cutlet – breaded pork chop, served hot or cold

Cow peas – a type of black-eye pea

Cullenskink – A traditional Scottish soup typically from Northern Scotland. Cullen is a Scottish village

Cumin seeds – pungent and aromatic spice used whole or ground

Glossary and interesting stuff

Curds – an Indian/English word for yoghurt, typically made at home

Curry leaves – this fragrant ingredient is commonly used in Southern Indian cookery

Desi ghee – see clarified butter. This is traditionally used in North India. It was seen as a luxury item (an expensive commodity) many years ago but is now widely used

Dippy egg – soft boiled egg

Dodo – a fried plantain

Duff – baked pudding and custard

Finny haddock – is the name we gave to smoked haddock

Folding – a baking method used in cake making. The action of folding is to use a metal spoon to gently cut through the cake mixture repeatedly to incorporate more air to make the cake as light as possible

Frikadellan – German type of faggot with minced pigs lungs made into meat balls, oven baked and eaten hot or cold

Garam masala – combination of aromatic spices

Gluten – is a protein found within wheat

Gram flour – flour derived from chick peas

Hoy-in – North East UK word – chuck, throw, put, place in

Kaffir lime leaves – often used in Asian cookery, can add depth and flavour to food

Kartoffel salad – vinegar based potato salad topped with herbs, very popular in Germany

Knead – to pull and push the dough from the outside in until the dough becomes more stretchy and glutinous

Knock back – in bread making, to knead out some of the built-up gases within the dough

Linseeds – give bread a nutty texture

Parmo – a fillet of chicken flattened out with a tenderising hammer, topped with cheese sauce then breadcrumbs, cooked until crispy. Eaten in the North East

Pattie – in and surrounding Hull 'pattie' is a herbed mashed potato in batter and deep fried. Only ever found in chip shops the 'pattie buttie' is a delicacy of Hull Town

Parboil – to part boil something e.g. potatoes prior to roasting so they become soft in the middle

Pease pudding – North East of England dish. Consisting of boiled split peas – pureed and chilled. Served hot or cold, it's nice with cooked ham in a stottie bread cake

Pie, mash and licker – pie and mash served with liquor (or licker) made from stewed eels and traditionally served in Essex and London regions

Plantain – an all year round staple food which can be used at any stage of ripeness. Like a banana but used like a potato

Prove – in bread making, to let dough rise in a warm place

Pulse – this is an action on a blender. You press the pulse button when you want your ingredients to break down in larger chunks, rather than blend until ingredients become a runny consistency

Raita – a cooling yoghurt side dish for curries, often made using cucumber

Ramadan – is the ninth month of the Islamic calendar. You fast from sunrise till sunset. It's festive month. When you open your fast you open it with one fruit date and a glass of water. A table would be full of different tasty dishes, but it's amazing how you can't eat much because you're so used to fasting

You try to do all good deeds in this month, and ask for forgiveness. I was told that this month teaches you of how people suffer around the world in poor countries when they don't have much to eat ever, and we find it difficult just in a day

It's also nice in this month when you socialise more with your friends by asking them to come and open their fast with you. At the end of the month we celebrate Eid (Christmas). This would be a day where we would make special dishes for everyone to come and share this day with us

Most of the month is about fasting but also about looking forward to eating and spoiling yourself with a variety of food and special expensive dishes that you wouldn't cook every day

Ras el Hanoot – a mixed Moroccan spice containing ingredients such as cumin, cinnamon, ground ginger and rose petals

Rest – in bread making, resting the dough helps it to rise which will help improve the quality of the bread

Glossary and interesting stuff

Rock eel and chips – rock eel or rock salmon are names that refer to a number of small sharks found in the Western Atlantic. It is a commonly sold in fish and chip shops in the UK. The firm pink-to-grey flesh keeps its texture when cooked and flakes easily It has a big spine running along the length of it covered in batter and you eat the fish around the spine

Roux – is the basis of making a white sauce. You can add cheese and prawns (as on page 91) or it can be varied for other sauces such as parsley, lemon etc

Saffron – a spice from the stigma of the crocus flower. The stigma is dried. The stigma strands are both pungent and colourful and are used to colour (golden yellow) and flavour food

Salt fish – is a white fish which is preserved in salt. Before you cook this you need to soak it in water to drain the salt out 24hrs before. You would normally grill it or put it in sauce to poach. It has a non-offensive taste if drained, soaked and rinsed correctly

Sarnie – is a sandwich

Sauerkraut – German coleslaw made from chopped or shredded cabbage salted and fermented in its own juice

Saveloy dip – a kind of soft sausage with a thin skin on it which is put in a bread bun that is smothered in pease pudding and dipped in a hot onion gravy then eaten hot. It can be eaten cold but better when warm as the saveloy sausage melts into your mouth. Eaten in the North East, especially South Shields

Sauté – a French term – to fry lightly

Schnitzel – thin 'escalope' of meat, usually veal or pork that is first floured, eggwashed then breadcrumbed before frying. It originated from Germany

Scouse – a stew from Liverpool made with beef or lamb

Seal – to fry something – like meat quickly to brown and retain the flavours

Shashlik – Russian/Turkish dish of cubes of different meat on a skewer served with spiced or curried sauce

Soldiers – fingers of toast or bread to dip into your egg

Spud – potato

Stottie cake – big round bread cob from North East England

Stottie pizza – a large bun called a stottie with tomato purée topped with cheese, bacon and mushrooms, popular in the North East

Tapioca milk pudding – we used to call this frog spawn

Tea cake – in Barnsley this is the name for a bread bun which is either plain or contains sultanas

Tawa – pronounced Tava. A black flat pan used for making flat bread such as chapattis

Tiddy Oggie – Cornish pasty

Translucent – becoming soft and see-through

Turmeric – a strong flavoured Indian spice which is a deep orangey/yellow in powder form

Vienna schnitzel – a traditional Austrian dish made with boneless meat, either pork or veal, thinned with a hammer, coated in breadcrumbs and fried

Wet Nellie – a sweet pastry pie, using stale cake crumbs and egg as the filling

Wok – a deep frying pan often used in Asian cooking

Acknowledgements

I owe a huge 'Thank You' to everyone who has been involved with this project – helping to turn my initial idea of linking mental and physical health and education with stories of recovery into this fabulous illustrated book.

Nourishing: Recipes and Reflections on Recovery reflects the personal recipes and memories of a diverse range of people, so first and foremost I must thank these key contributors – the service users, patients, staff and carers of Nottinghamshire Healthcare NHS Trust who entrusted their special memories to my care.

Secondly, I'd like to thank the Trust's Chief Executives and Senior Managers, who have supported me throughout: they listened to my outline plans and provided the resources for me to undertake the project.

There are many other people within the Trust to thank: my manager and the Communications Team, the Senior Dietitian, Research Lead for Forensic Division and the Catering Managers, all of whom have given generously of their time and support; also all the ward, therapy and day unit based staff who have helped enormously in facilitating the project.

And now, thanks to all those people outside the Trust who have made valuable contributions in many different ways: to Michelin starred chef and restaurateur Sat Bains; Dr Nuri Gene-Cos; Dr Julie Repper; Jo Cook; and my lecturers at the University of Nottingham.

I feel tremendously fortunate to have worked with Dick Makin Imaging. Dick and Jo have guided me throughout the production of the book – the photography, food styling, design, layout and editing. Thank you so much for your ideas and your tireless energy and enthusiasm.

And last but not least, my thanks to all my friends and family, particularly my mum and my sister who have helped out with photo shoots, and my husband and children who have been extremely tolerant of my busy schedule.

Nourishing book Nottinghamshire Healthcare NHS Trust 2012
Text and concept Helen Ashwell 2012
Photography, design, layout Dick Makin 2012 www.dmimaging.co.uk
ISBN: 978 0 904327 05 2
Printed: Ruddocks, Lincoln www.ruddocks.co.uk
Published: Ruddocks Publishing Ltd, Lincoln